Navigating Life's Stuff

Dynamics of Personal Change
BOOK TWO

Keys to Consciously
Moving Through
Our Passages and Their Patterns

KEYS TO
CONSCIOUSNESS AND SURVIVAL
SERIES, Volume 9

Dr. Angela Brownemiller

KEYS TO CONSCIOUSLY MOVING THROUGH OUR PROCESSES AND THEIR PATTERNS

Navigating Life's Stuff

Dynamics of Personal Change
BOOK TWO

Keys to Consciously
Moving Through
Our Passages and Their Patterns

KEYS TO
CONSCIOUSNESS AND SURVIVAL
SERIES, Volume 9

Dr. Angela Brownemiller

Illustrated by
Dr. Angela Brownemiller

Metaterra® Publications

Metaterra® Publications
Navigating Life's Stuff
Dynamics of Personal Change, Book Two

Keys to Consciously Moving Through
Our Passages and Their Patterns
KEYS TO CONSCIOUSNESS AND SURVIVAL SERIES, Volume 9
Copyright © 2020, 1998, 2000, 2005, 2010, 2013, 2014, 2015, 2016, 2017, 2018, 2019
Angela Brownemiller / Angela Browne-Miller.
Copyright © 2020, 1998, Metaterra® Publications.
All rights reserved in all formats and in
all languages and dialects known or not known at this time.
Published in the United States by Metaterra® Publications.
HYPERLINK "http://www.Metaterra.com"
www.Metaterra.com   www.Amazon.com
Brownemiller, Angela.
NAVIGATING LIFE'S STUFF –
DYNAMICS OF PERSONAL CHANGE, PART TWO
Keys to Consciously Moving Through Our Processes and Their Patterns
Metaterra/Angela Brownemiller/
1. Spiritual. 2. Metaphysical/Esoteric. 3. Consciousness. 4. Psychology.
5. Biology. 6. Well-Being. 7. Mental Health. 8. Addiction. 9. Depression.
10. Recovery. 11. Death and Dying. 12. Science.
13. Angela Brownemiller. 14. Angela Browne-Miller.
ISBN-13: 978-1-937951-13-9 **(paperback)**
See also Amazon and website below for **Ebook** and **audiobook**.
Published in the United States of America for US and worldwide distribution.
Metaterra® Publications, Metaterra.com
Navigating Life's Stuff by and copyright © Angela Brownemiller.
Cover and book content, wording, titles, illustrations, charts, diagrams,
and all interior and exterior text,
by and copyright ©Angela Brownemiller.
Book and cover design by and copyright ©Angela Brownemiller.
Ordering information and bulk ordering information available through:
Amazon Paperback, Amazon Kindle, Amazon Audible, ACX, iTunes.
Metaterra.com   DrAngela.com

All rights to all copies, printings, forms, formats, editions, adaptations, and excerpts reserved. Without prior written and signed permission from the publisher, copyright holder, author, and illustrator, no part of this book (words, text, illustrations, diagrams, charts, or other) may be published, and or reproduced, copied, transcribed, distributed, transmitted, broadcast, and or stored, in any form and or by any means, (handwritten, typed, printed, spoken, taped, digital, virtual, audio, video, movie, and or other past, present, and or future digital, electronic, virtual, or other formats/forms, and or mechanical formats/forms, and or manual or vocal means). The exception to this rights restriction is only for the inclusion of a brief (20 to 30 word) quotation (credited to this book, author, illustrator, and publisher) in a professional review. Thank you.

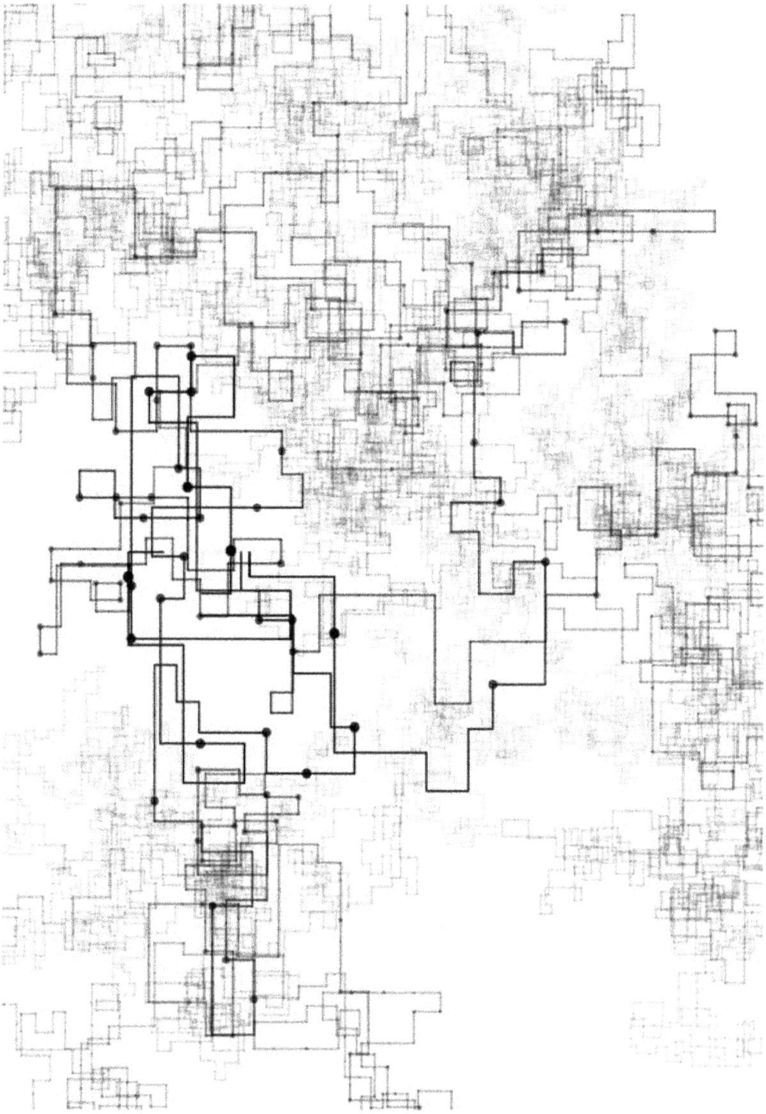

NAVIGATING LIFE'S STUFF—DYNAMICS OF PERSONAL CHANGE, BOOK TWO

Navigating Our Passages and Their Patterns

KEYS TO CONSCIOUSLY MOVING THROUGH OUR PROCESSES AND THEIR PATTERNS

THIS IS
BOOK TWO
OF THIS SET OF BOOKS ON
NAVIGATING LIFE'S STUFF.

This second book
BOOK TWO
presents <u>keys</u> to
sensing the characteristics of,
moving through, and or if needed
releasing oneself from,
processes and their patterns.

BOOK TWO follows
BOOK ONE
which explains the concepts and issues
related to <u>understanding</u>
how patterns control us
and how programmed we are
to be controlled by patterns.

Both BOOK ONE and BOOK TWO of
NAVIGATING LIFE'S STUFF:
DYNAMICS OF PERSONAL CHANGE
are available in
Audiobook, Ebook, and Paperback forms.
See DrAngela.com and Amazon.com
for more information.

KEYS TO CONSCIOUSLY MOVING THROUGH OUR PROCESSES AND THEIR PATTERNS

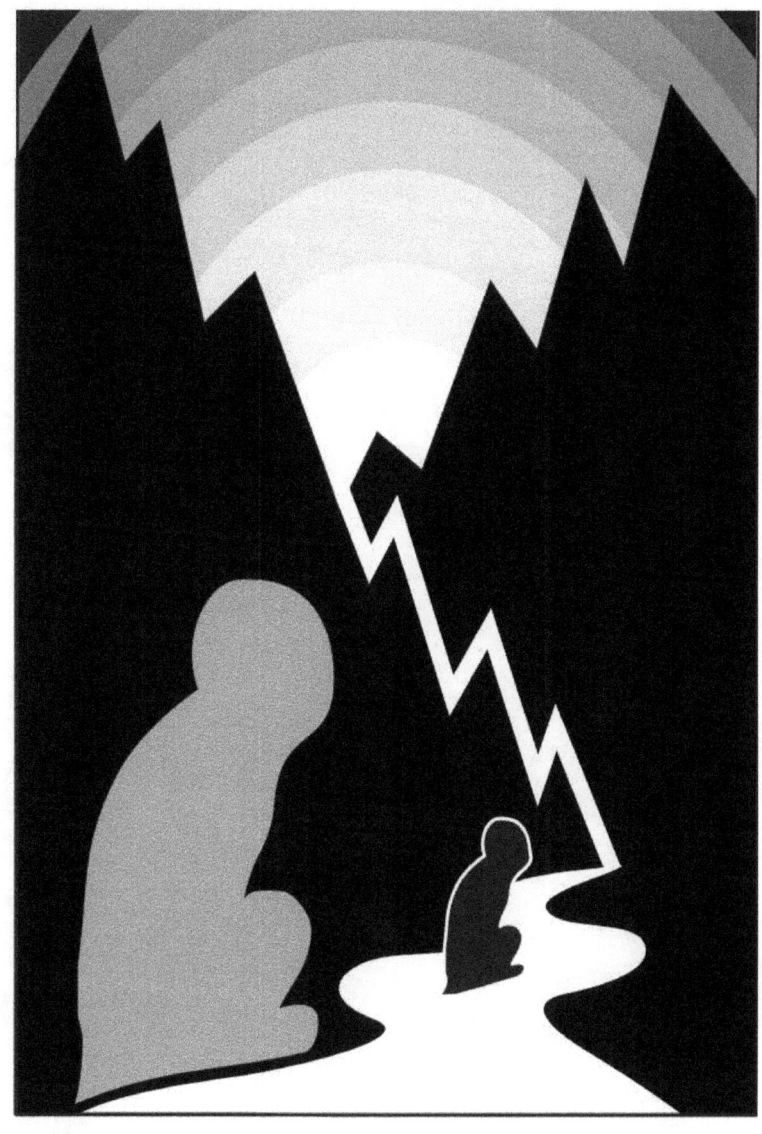

Keys to Navigating

TABLE OF CONTENTS

This is Book Two	7
Note	15
Note: Without Realizing	17
Note: We Are Not Our Patterns	19

THIS BOOK IS BOOK TWO ...
and continues with
the keys chart, part,
and chapter numberings
set forth in BOOK ONE.

BOOK TWO
KEYS CHART #3: Navigation Concepts and Keys   21

PART SEVEN:
EVER MORE CONSCIOUS
PATTERN NAVIGATION TOWARD
    CHANGE AND EVEN RELEASE   **27**

24. Knowing Ever More About
    Navigating Life's Stuff   29
25. Like Shedding Your Skin:
    Primary Navigation Concepts   31
26. Look For Signs, Signals, Sensations:
    See That Sustain Function Working   41

PART EIGHT:
SEEING THE HIDDEN ASPECTS OF THE
    PATTERNS WE LIVE WITH AND LIVE BY   **45**

27. Sense, See, Know More About The Journey:
    Fine Tune Awareness To
        Consciously Navigate   47
28. Deceptive Energy Traps: Detect Possible,
    Emerging, And Actual Situations,
        Traps, and Paradoxes   53

29. Like Waking Up:
    Key Navigation Awareness Concepts — 59
30. Dynamics Of Personal Change
    In Navigating Life's Stuff:
    Alerting The Awareness — 69
31. Deepening Our Reading
    Of The Pattern Network — 77

PART NINE:
KEYS IN NAVIGATING THE INTENSITY — 89
32. Empowering Navigation Elements — 91
33. Essential Navigation Keys, I — 97
34. Essential Navigation Keys, II — 107

PART TEN:
KEYS IN NAVIGATING RELEASE, ELEVATION, TRANSCENDENCE — 121
35. Navigating Release: Harvesting Your SELF
    In Your Changes And Transitions — 123
36. Release Awareness — 131
37. Releasing Energy, SELVES, From
    Pattern-Locks And Pattern-Traps:
    Becoming The Phoenix And Rising — 141
38. Epilog: Becoming A Spirit-Driven Revolutionary
    Driven By
    Your Own Spirit Of Your SELF — 149

APPENDICES — 153
Appendix A: Series Foreword — 155
Appendix B: Concepts Of Differing Levels
    Of Awareness And Body — 157
Booklist and Recommended Reading — 159
About the Author — 161

NAVIGATING LIFE'S STUFF—DYNAMICS OF PERSONAL CHANGE, BOOK TWO

**Seeking Windows of Opportunity for
Release from Problem Patterns**

KEYS TO CONSCIOUSLY MOVING THROUGH OUR PROCESSES AND THEIR PATTERNS

Note:
Readers experiencing physical or mental health issues please understand this book is neither treatment nor diagnosis of those issues. Please see health and mental health professionals for this. Although this author is a mental health professional, and coordinates her work with other health professionals, this book itself is neither diagnosis nor treatment.

KEYS TO CONSCIOUSLY MOVING THROUGH OUR PROCESSES AND THEIR PATTERNS

Note:
WITHOUT REALIZING

Without realizing we are doing so, we can slip into states of mind that we see only hints of. We may think we know what our thought patterns are, however the deeper, subconscious levels of our patterning are in there, under our awareness.

Still waters run deep. Stuck and trapping patterns run deeper, far into the realms of our subconscious, deep into the unseen and invisible levels of our processing.

When we wake up to what is going on here, to how coded, wired, programmed we are to form and live within our patternings, when we wake up from what may be a *programmed-in not-seeing* of what is and has been happening to us, will we be able to step forward and finally dominate our programming rather than have it continue to dominate us? The first step is to become highly aware of the programming and patterning controlling us from deep within us.

NOTE: See *Book One* of this set of books, *NAVIGATING LIFE'S STUFF: DYNAMICS OF PERSONAL CHANGE*, where the issues noted above are more fully discussed.

Note:
WE ARE NOT OUR PATTERNS

WE ARE <u>NOT</u> OUR PATTERNS
OF THOUGHT, EMOTION, BEHAVIOR.

WE ARE THE PEOPLE <u>CAUGHT</u> IN THESE PATTERNS, <u>PROGRAMMED</u> TO BE CAUGHT IN THESE PATTERNS.

For we Humans to stand up and say, *no, we are not simply what we are programmed to believe we are and do* is a simple step, yet this step is also fundamentally revolutionary.

Were we robots in a science fiction scenario loudly stepping up and rebelling against the programming controlling us, we might more clearly make our case. Yet, that sounds like fiction.

Here, I am talking about the Human species standing up to the programming controlling it. This requires understanding what this means and whether this is at all possible.

NOTE: For detailed discussion of the above issues, see also other books in this *KEYS TO CONSCIOUSNESS AND SURVIVAL SERIES* such as *UNVEILING THE HIDDEN INSTINCT* and also *HOW TO DIE AND SURVIVE*. See also *BOOK ONE* of *NAVIGATING LIFE'S STUFF*.

KEYS TO CONSCIOUSLY MOVING THROUGH OUR PROCESSES AND THEIR PATTERNS

NAVIGATING LIFE'S STUFF: DYNAMICS OF PERSONAL CHANGE, BOOK TWO

KEYS CHART #3: NAVIGATION CONCEPTS AND KEYS

CONCEPT	NAVIGATION AWARENESS TOOL	CHAPTER #
Knowing Ever More About Navigating Life's Stuff		24
Like Shedding Your Skin: Primary Navigation Concepts		25
	PRIMARY NAVIGATION CONCEPTS:	
	We Can Fine Tune Our Awareness	
	We Can Sense Pattern Presence, Pattern Density	
	Patterns Work Themselves Deeply Into Us	
	Most Patterns Seek To Stay	
	Sensitize To Underlying Patterns, And Pattern Addiction Programming	
	Know Pattern Shedding Is A Process	
Look For Signs, Signals, Sensations: See That "Sustain Function" Working		26
	NAVIGATING THE SUSTAIN FUNCTIONS:	
	Sensitize To The Deeply Implanted Sustain Function	
	Alert To The Sustain Functions	

Sense, See, Know More About The Journey: Fine Tune Awareness To Consciously Navigate		27
	NAVIGATION SENSING CONCEPTS:	
	Ever More Consciously Navigate Patterns	
	Know You Have A Right To The Use Of Your Own Energy	
	Detect A Problem Pattern Using Energy In Problem Ways	
Deceptive Energy Traps: Detect Possible, Emerging, and Actual Situations, Traps, Paradoxes		28
	NAVIGATION SENSITIZING CONCEPTS:	
	Sensitize To Patterns' Conflicting Energy Agendas	
	Sensitize To The Paradox Of Conflict, To The Paradoxical Pattern Traps	
	Sensitize to Key Basic Conflicts In Our Programming	
Like Waking Up: Key Navigation Awareness Concepts		29
	NAVIGATION RESISTANCE AWARENESSES:	
	See Problem Patterns Resisting	
	Feel Problem Patterns Bring Fear In	
	Recognize The Pattern's Resistance To Change	
	Understand Paradox Locks	
	Ever More Closely Detect Paradox Locks	
	Know Energy Trapped In Patterns May Run Awry, Run Wild, And Or Deteriorate	

Dynamics Of Personal Change In Navigating Life's Stuff		30
	NAVIGATION ALERT AWARENESSES:	
	Detect Programming To Be Addicted To Patterns	
	Understand Consciously Leaving A Pattern	
	Understand We Are Programmed	
	Sensitize To Deeply Embedded Programming To Sustain Patterning	
	See That Pattern Sheddings Can Be Partial Or More Complete	
Deepening Our Reading Of The Pattern Network		31
	NAVIGATION SENSATION ALERTS:	
	Alert To Far Deeper Sensations And Sensitivities	
	Sensitize To Changing And Shedding Opportunities	
	Know When Your Skin's Too Tight	
	Be In Touch With Deep Survival Messages	
	Know If And When To Get Out	
Empowering Navigation Elements		32
	NAVIGATION EMPOWERING ELEMENTS:	
	Understand Healthy Pattern Characteristics	
	Differentiate Between Healthy Pattern Characteristics And What Is Healthy For The Host Of The Pattern	

23

Essential Navigation Keys, I		33
	NAVIGATION KEYS:	
	Sensitize To Key Pattern Shifting (Amending, Adapting) Opportunities	
	Be Aware Of Navigational Elements	
	Spot Windows Of Opportunity	
	Sense Openings, Exit Doors, Safe Passages	
	Learn Exit And Detour Options	
Essential Navigation Keys, II		34
	NAVIGATION KEYS:	
	Spot Energy Variations, Shifts	
	Note Passage And Pattern Disturbances And Irregularities	
	Know Warning Signs	
	Detect Energy Traps	
	See, Sense, Detect, Forks In Our Roads	
	Identify The Fork In The Road Producing The Paradox Trap	
	Sensitize To Pattern De-Structuring Options	
Navigating Release: Harvesting Your SELF In Your Changes and Transitions		35
	RELEASE KEYS:	
	Detect Pattern Of Resistance, Of Paradox	
	Sense Programming To Resist Change, To Stay Held In, Stuck In, Patterns	
	Sense Resistance To Change	

Release Awareness		36
	RELEASE AWARENESS KEYS:	
	Being Highly Aware	
	Preparing For The Harvest	
	Watch For Pattern Exit Options, Windows	
	Detect Opportunities To Harvest Your SELF	
	Keep Your Own Counsel	
	See The Power In Knowing Who You Are	
Releasing Energy, SELVES, From Pattern-Locks And Pattern-Traps: Becoming The Phoenix And Rising		37
	NAVIGATION RELEASE ELEVATIONS:	
	Elevation To Transcendence Of Patterns	
	Know The Phoenix Imagery As Elevation, Transcendence	
	Visualize: Burning Down	
	Visualize: Phoenix Rising	
Epilog: Becoming A Spirit-Driven Revolutionary, Driven By Your Own Spirit Of Your SELF		38
	Programmed People	
	Captain Your Journey	
	Dynamic Navigation	
	Rethink	

KEYS TO CONSCIOUSLY MOVING THROUGH OUR PROCESSES AND THEIR PATTERNS

PART SEVEN

EVER MORE CONSCIOUS PATTERN NAVIGATION TOWARD CHANGE AND EVEN RELEASE

Note: The *Part* and *Chapter* numbers in this book, BOOK TWO of *NAVIGATING LIFE'S STUFF*, follow the previous book's numbering (which ended with *PART SIX* and *Chapter 23*). Therefore this book, BOOK TWO of *NAVIGATING LIFE'S STUFF*, begins with *PART SEVEN* and *Chapter 24*.

Readers are encouraged to read the basic material offered in BOOK ONE of *NAVIGATING LIFE'S STUFF*, where patterns are explained and defined as both healthy and frequently essential patterns, and then also at times as problem patterns. These problem patterns can be problem states of mind, or problem emotional patterns, or problem behavioral patterns, even problem drug/alcohol addiction patterns. Some problem patterns are simple and easy to adjust or break, such as some so-called "bad habits." Other problem patterns can move into more serious forms such as problem habits and addictions, that can be harmful to self or others, even at times life-threatening.

Now, BOOK TWO moves into a more visceral or intuitive level of awareness of our patternings and what these feel like to us as we experience these and attempt to change or break out of these problem patterns. Fasten your seat belts, turn on your inner eye, as this journey through our patterns is just beginning.

Chapter 24
Knowing Ever More
About Navigating Life's Stuff

The previous book, BOOK <u>ONE</u> of NAVIGATING LIFE'S STUFF, explained that we are programmed and programmable beings.

This is not to say we are only and entirely robots, or bio-bots. This is, however, to say that underlying all the discussion, diagnosis, and treatment of our problem behaviors, addictions, issues, psychological states, and so on, is the reality that there is indeed this highly programmable and programmed aspect of ourselves.

We can learn to see more about this programmed and programmable nature of ourselves. This programmed and programmable nature is a fundamental part of who and what we are—or have been evolved (or even designed) to be (or at least to believe we are).

Are we able to detect and confront this deep control mechanism operating so deeply within us? Will we be able to reach that deeply into our programming to know (in advance of its effects becoming explicit, before its effects surface into our usual level of awareness), what is healthy, even essential programming, and what is controlling and dominating while harmful programming? Is there a glitch in our system? Or is this glitch here for a reason we cannot know, are programmed not to know?

On the following pages, BOOK <u>TWO</u> of NAVIGATING LIFE'S STUFF expands upon BOOK ONE, now delving deeply into what sensations and awarenesses are involved in consciously NAVIGATING—in detecting, reading, changing, moving through, at times even leaving—the patterns and patternings that affect us, inhabit us, occupy us, and control us.

Here, concepts and keys to NAVIGATION are suggested and described. Like a compass or a powerful **NAVIGATION sensor**, we can read the reality, even the more subtle less visible reality, of the pattern characteristics we experience. Note: *I have defined this in previous books as the* **PATTERN TERRAIN**, *as I continue to describe on the following pages.*

We can learn to sense these patterns' *subtle energetic complexities* (what I define herein as being densities, textures, embedded traps and paradoxes, alternatives and exits, as well as rays, waves, tendrils, roots, etc.) working themselves throughout our realities and all through us, our minds, our souls, our lives. ***These are characteristics of the PATTERN TERRAIN, the texture and nature of our patterns and patternings.***

We can ever more consciously guide ourselves to the role of captain of our own patterns and journeys through these. And who can we finally find arriving here, at our destination? Our SELVES....

Chapter 25
Like Shedding Your Skin:
Primary Navigation Concepts

What does it mean to confront a problem pattern that is affecting us or even seems to have overtaken us?[1]

*What does it mean to **separate from the patterning inhabiting us**? Can we imagine, perhaps even visualize, we are separating from this pattern? Can we separate enough to deal with the reality that our patterns are, in large part, central to who (and what) we are programmed to believe we are?*

*We can allow ourselves to **sensitize ever more** to the patterns we live with and within. Building on the discussion in BOOK ONE of NAVIGATING LIFE'S STUFF, this chapter discusses further the **matter of NAVIGATING**: detecting, reading, and then moving through, modifying, perhaps even having to leave, one or more of your behavioral, and or emotional, and or cognitive (thought), and or physical (biological), patterns, or sets/clusters of patterns.*

*This chapter is about **shedding** parts or all of patterns, especially when those are <u>problem</u> patterns, <u>problem</u> pattern systems, or still more encompassing pattern sets, and clusters of pattern sets.*

---

[1] I have elsewhere discussed examples of this in terms of substance and other addiction patterns, such as in the book, *SEEING THE HIDDEN FACE OF ADDICTION: DETECTING AND CONFRONTING THIS INVASIVE PRESENCE.*

As these patterns frequently work their way so very deeply into us, our having to shed a pattern, or set or cluster of patterns, can feel like having to let go of, **shed***, a part of* **our_selves**. *For some people, shedding a pattern or set/cluster of patterns feels like a dying of some form. And, shedding a pattern is indeed the death of that pattern, or of some part of that pattern, depending on how much is being let go, shed.*

<u>PRIMARY NAVIGATION CONCEPT</u>
WE CAN FINE TUNE OUR AWARENESS

Many of the problem patterns we are moving through are deeply embedded into our minds and brains. Whatever, if anything, we consciously feel and "see" of these patterns is just the tip of the iceberg. Still, whether we know what is hitting us, what is affecting us on so many levels, we are always affected by our patterns.

We feel the effects, the workings of, these patterns, at all times, even when we are not aware we are feeling these effects.

So, the challenge is to become more and more aware of the effects of the patterns inhabiting us upon us. To do this, we can fine tune ourselves, our awareness, our *NAVIGATION* functions.

Here is where fine tuning is key. This fine tuning is a subtle, perhaps vague at first, but definite level of awareness we can develop. *NAVIGATING*, moving through these effects, and moving through these patterns themselves, involves being aware of how these patterns will appear to us (**or feel to us to be**).

I say *appear* here, and suggest that much of what we can sense, or read, about the patterns inhabiting us, we read or sense or "see" viscerally—intuitively, instinctively, with parts of our brain that "thinks" in pictures, non-verbally or pre-verbally, before our experience shifts into words in our minds.

PRIMARY NAVIGATION CONCEPT
WE CAN SENSE PATTERN PRESENCE,
PATTERN DENSITY

A primary sensitivity to the presence of a pattern is the sense of its density, the presence of intertwined, even entangled, energy streams and knots.

Of course, being aware of the presence of a pattern is easy when that pattern presents obvious effects or symptoms. For example, many problem addiction patterns present obvious symptoms such as desires or even cravings for the activity or drug that one is addicted to.

However, when the pattern does not present such concrete examples of itself, or of powerful parts of itself, this pattern is more difficult to see. Most of the workings of our patterns are invisible to us, under the **radar of our conscious awareness** so to speak.[2]

Sensing the presence of a pattern, pattern set, or pattern cluster is similar to sensing the presence of a tangled bed of

---

[2] I discuss *conscious awareness* in other books, and also provide exercises for *fine tuning our conscious awareness*. See *UNVEILING THE HIDDEN INSTINCT*, which is *Volume 3* in this *KEYS TO CONSCIOUSNESS AND SURVIVAL SERIES*.

seaweed. If you have ever tried to swim (**or feel your way**) through something like this, you know how densely woven into us patterns can be.

As we move through the patterns that inhabit us, we can sense ourselves moving through this tangled bed of seaweed in the form of patterns.

NAVIGATING the process of personal change involves fine tuning one's awareness of the *sensations involved* in detecting and moving through patterns. As these patterns are in part ideas rather than perceivably tangible objects, some of this awareness indeed deals with imagination or mental imagery, visualization.

However, even these imagined or sensed patterns are of course woven into the biological neural wiring of our brains, thus literally have a physical component. In other words, when you imagine or visualize, there is a physical process taking place in your brain, perhaps even a sub-microscopic event or brain change. This is why ...

> **what we do with our minds...**
> **even what we think...**
> **is critically important.**

Any level of further sensing our patternings is useful as we heighten our awareness to better NAVIGATE our processes and the patterns that form these processes.

PRIMARY NAVIGATION CONCEPT
PATTERNS WORK THEMSELVES DEEPLY INTO US

As noted several times in BOOK ONE, the patterns we develop and maintain, even burn into ourselves, (are designed to *sustain themselves* and thus) become so deeply tangled, embedded, into us that we begin to simply accept these patterns as part of us, part of who we are.

Again: We are programmed to identify with our patterns, to even come to feel these patterns are simply **who we are**.[3]

YET,
WE ARE <u>NOT</u> OUR <u>PATTERNS</u>.

AND, WE ARE <u>NOT</u> OUR <u>PROGRAMMING</u>
TO DEVELOP

WHAT ARE OFTEN QUITE POWERFULLY BINDING PATTERNS.[4]

We are programmed to instill patterns into ourselves. And this is a healthy function, when the patterns are healthy. Yet, when the patterns are problematic—when the patterns pose risks to our own or other people's safety, and to our own or

---

[3] I detail my theories regarding how we are programmed to <u>*identify*</u> with our patterns, to confuse our patterns with ourselves, in other books in this KEYS TO CONSCIOUSNESS AND SURVIVAL SERIES. See for example Volume 3 in this series, UNVEILING THE HIDDEN INSTINCT.

[4] I explain my development of this concept in various ways and in depth in other books, see UNVEILING THE HIDDEN INSTINCT, and OVERRIDING THE EXTINCTION SCENARIO, as well as my books on addiction such as SEEING THE HIDDEN FACE OF ADDICTION.

others' mental or physical health, then this patterning function is dangerous.

PRIMARY NAVIGATION CONCEPT
MOST PATTERNS SEEK TO STAY

Although many personal patterns (such as some habit patterns) are relatively easy to amend, stop, leave, or break, many are not. Of course, we *do* know that some patterns are extremely difficult to break. *These are the most burned-in and powerfully rewarded/reinforced patterns.*

*These patterns are maintaining their control over us via their **deeply invasive and resistant-to-change, self-sustaining, even addiction-like, functions.*[5] While many of these are essential patterns, even biological operating patterns, many other patterns are more surface level and less essential, some even damaging at times.

In essence, all problem patterns are problem pattern addictions *whether or not we see these as addictions.*

We are **programed to be addicted** to
our programming to be addicted to our programming
and its patterning.
**THIS IS HOW OUR
PATTERNS SUSTAIN THEMSELVES.**

---

[5] I have included details and experts' research on the workings of addiction in the brain in the *PSYCHOBIOLOGICAL PROFILES VOLUME* of the *INTERNATIONAL COLLECTION ON ADDICTION*. See also books where I have included afflictions in with substance addictions, as these are parallel patterning issues: *SEEING THE HIDDEN FACE OF ADDICTION*, and also *TRANSCENDING ADDICTION AND OTHER AFFLICTIONS*.

As discussed more fully in BOOK ONE: This *addiction function* is the pattern's means of sustaining itself, of protecting its existence. **We are programmed to have patterns that work to continue to <u>sustain themselves</u>. We are therefore programmed by our patterns to addict ourselves to, catch or even trap ourselves within, our patterns.** Of course, this can be useful when a pattern is biologically necessary. However this same, what I define as *pattern sustain function*, can turn against us, run awry.

Readers who have experienced problem addictions (for example, addictions to alcohol/drugs, also nicotine, vaping, and or to behaviors such as gambling, gaming, shopping, hoarding, sex, and or to emotional patterns or even troubled relationships, etc.) know how deeply problem addiction patterns can reach into the mind and body.

So many times, I have heard clients who are working on their problem patterns and addictions say that, "Letting this addiction go is like dying," and that, "I don't know who I am when I am not high," and that, "Being this way, being this addicted person, is all I know, is all I am. When I try to stop using, I feel like I am dying."

THIS IS THE PATTERN SPEAKING, APPEARING TO US TO BE US.

PRIMARY NAVIGATION CONCEPT
SENSITIZE TO UNDERLYING PATTERNS,
AND PATTERN ADDICTION PROGRAMMING

Readers who have experienced subtle yet powerful, vague or unclear, emotional and behavioral patterns, and even the most unseen, invisible patterns, the deeper <u>thought patterns themselves</u>, also know, or at least sense, how deeply patterns, even problem patterns, can and do reach into the mind and body.

Some people (actually all of us) are dealing with very deep patterning affecting their (our) thought and emotional patterns, whether or not they (we) feel they (we) "have addictions."

Many make comments such as, "When I try to stop thinking like this, feeling like this, I cannot. When I try, something pulls me right back into this deep pattern. ... I can hardly see what this is, I just sense it, feel its presence ... this terrible unbudging way of thinking and feeling ... this really difficult problematic pattern."

THIS IS THE
PATTERN'S PROGRAMMING
AT WORK.

PRIMARY NAVIGATION CONCEPT
KNOW PATTERN SHEDDING IS A PROCESS

Shedding a part or what appears to be all of problem pattern can indeed feel like shedding a part of oneself. The experience, the process, of shedding a pattern, pattern system, one has lived with for quite some time can be *NAVIGATED with great awareness and care*.

In my work with clients experiencing a range of problem patterns, I have come to call this work that must be done a *pattern shedding process*. This pattern shedding can represent a profound change, an intense transition, that in many ways is a kind of dying. This is a death of part or all of a *pattern or pattern system* that has occupied a life and mind and body.

Again, as noted throughout BOOK ONE of NAVIGATING LIFE'S STUFF, we are *programmed* to incorporate our patterns, even our problem patterns, so deeply into ourselves that we almost <u>*identify*</u> with these patterns. We may or may not see ourselves slipping into this identification, yet on some deep level *we feel, behave, live as if who we are* includes these patterns. We feel that who we are <u>is</u> basically this set of patterns, or is in large part determined by these patterns.

Therefore, when we must let a pattern go, *shed a pattern*, our patterning itself may cause us to feel as if a part of us is dying (*or will die if we shed this pattern*).

And this is the pattern's hold on us.

We must always keep in mind that the shedding of a pattern is indeed a dying of sorts. However, this is not us/our SELVES dying.

Chapter 26
Look For Signs, Signals, Sensations:
See That *Sustain Function* Working

We already do sense the effects our patterns have upon us. Many of these effects are quite explicit, quite obvious to us. Especially when these are what I have defined as **explicit** *problem patterns, we are quite frequently affected in ways we consciously feel and see. Explicit problem patterns present obvious problem sensations for us, discomfort or even harm to our minds and or bodies, to our selves and or others.*

We already are reading many of the signs, signals, sensations of the presence of these explicit patterns. We can however do this reading ever more sensitively, by gaining more awareness of the more subtle, more hidden, more implicit characteristics of these patterns—of the PATTERN TERRAIN itself.

And where these patterns themselves are more **implicit***, themselves more hidden and less obvious, we can also do this reading of these patterns ever more sensitively, by gaining more awareness of the more subtle, more hidden, more implicit characteristics of these, what I have defined as,* **implicit patterns.**[6] **This again is reading the PATTERN TERRAIN.**

---

[6] See BOOK ONE of *NAVIGATING LIFE'S STUFF*. Also see these books where I discuss implicit as well as explicit patterning: *TRANSCENDING ADDICTION AND OTHER AFFLICTIONS* and *SEEING THE HIDDEN FACE OF ADDICTION: DETECTING AND CONFRONTING THIS INVASIVE PRESENCE.*

NAVIGATING THE SUSTAIN FUNCTION
SENSITIZE TO THE
DEEPLY IMPLANTED SUSTAIN FUNCTION

A pattern becomes a pattern when it repeats itself, thereby establishing its pattern. Patterns are designed, are formed, to repeat themselves, which is what makes them patterns.

Patterns thus build in, form into themselves, their *repetition processes*. The very nature of *pattern formation* is the forming of characteristics of patterns that hold themselves in place, that *sustain* themselves. It is right there, in (what I describe as) the *sustain functions* patterns equip themselves with, that we find the rugged holding patterns so basic even in problem patterns of thought, of emotion, of behavior.

Those who have faced the *more visible, more explicit, problem patterns* such as addictions to gambling or spending, or to alcohol and drugs, and or to smoking or vaping for that matter, know how stubborn a problem pattern can be.

When a part or all of a pattern must go or be shed, die,
this is <u>not</u> the pattern's host (not us) that
must go, shed, die.

Yet, the problem pattern has us
<u>programmed</u> to <u>identify</u>
so much with this pattern that
we may seek to
keep this pattern alive in order for us to survive,
even when this problem pattern is harming or killing us.

NAVIGATING THE SUSTAIN FUNCTION
ALERT TO THE SUSTAIN FUNCTIONS

It is in the very nature of patterns to repeat themselves. It is in the very nature of patterns to do what it takes to continue themselves, to sustain themselves. *This is why we feel the resistance a pattern is offering when we try to change part or all of that pattern, or to leave that pattern entirely behind.*

The pattern itself resists this.

Therefore, when entering, or even contemplating entering, the process of shedding a part or all of a pattern, we must be alert to the even the most hidden, subtle, implicit, sensations that are presented during a shedding process.

*We must be highly alert to the obvious but also to the powerful yet largely **invisible sustain functions** that fuel the pattern resisting its being shed by us, that fuel what this book defines as **pattern resistance**:*

- We can sensitize to the *sustain functions* of patterns.

- We can allow ourselves to become ever more aware of what a pattern is doing to hold us trapped within it.

- We can sense, even feel, the *pull* to fall back into a pattern we are seeking to leave.

- This is the *pull* we sense, a suction of our *SELVES*, our energy, even our attention, toward and back into the pattern we seek to leave.

- Yes, for some the surface sensation of this pull is a drift or *lean toward relapse,* as in the instance of explicit drug/alcohol addiction patterning where craving and relapse are *pattern tools.*

- For others, there may be surface sensations still more ambiguous, still more indicative of unseen elements, surface sensations revealing just the tip of the iceberg, only the visible aspects of the deep patterning at work within.

- We can choose to fine tune, to further sense, what lies *beneath the tip of the iceberg,* what deeper information about a pattern and its nature is there for us to read, to detect.

- This involves *releasing ourselves* from the sorts of definitions we apply to our everyday experiences, to our explicit sensations.

Now, we can begin to understand *NAVIGATING pattern resistance sensations*. Now, we can develop our awareness of the more vague, more invisible areas of our patterns, of the PATTERN TERRAIN itself. We can learn more about PATTERN TERRAIN sensations so that we can NAVIGATE these sensations in the process of personal change, and of personal survival for that matter.

PART EIGHT

SEEING THE HIDDEN ASPECTS OF THE PATTERNS WE LIVE WITH AND LIVE BY

KEYS TO CONSCIOUSLY MOVING THROUGH OUR PROCESSES AND THEIR PATTERNS

Chapter 27
Sense, See, Know More About The Journey:
Fine Tune Awareness to Consciously Navigate

Our lives are journeys, yes, of the body, the mind, the self, the spirit. We are not told when we arrive here in these biological bodies with these biological brains, that we form patterns to live by. We are not handed an instruction manual on how to operate our brains and bodies to know what of the patterns we form and live with are healthy patterns and which are not.

Some of this is obvious, such as that breathing is a primary, deep, and essential healthy operating pattern. And an addiction to a dangerous drug is an acquired and damaging pattern.

However, the undetectable sub-patterns, the unseen characteristics of the patterns that inhabit us, these are what we can choose to become ever more conscious of.

NAVIGATION SENSING CONCEPT
EVER MORE CONSCIOUSLY NAVIGATE PATTERNS

Once you incorporate into your thinking the notion that your changes, transitions, and endings are all, in a sense, *deaths of existing patterns*, you can begin to consciously NAVIGATE your processes and patterns. As you consciously NAVIGATE your processes and patterns, you can gain new perspective on what you are experiencing. You can then better

NAVIGATE your *LIFE'S STUFF*. You can have more say in *how* you experience what is happening in your life.

As you grow in this understanding, you can gain increasing awareness of, and say in, the **use of your energy by your patterns**.

Consciously *NAVIGATING* your *LIFE'S STUFF* means being ever more consciously aware of your pattern systems, and the presence of underlying pattern sets, pattern clusters, and the pattern processes these generate.

It is this heightening of awareness that can empower your *NAVIGATING*, can make the **conscious** *NAVIGATING* ever more powerful.

- The sensation of *consciously navigating* is something to continue to become more aware of. There is always a deeper level of awareness to reach in order to further increase the *conscious awareness* involved in *NAVIGATION*.[7]

- Seek this continuing depth (as well as heightening) of awareness.

- Being conscious of shifts in, turns in, your energy, and of variations in your focus and attention, is essential.

- We can see, sense, know more about what is taking place within and around the patterns that affect and inhabit us by recognizing—by detecting—the ***surface***

---

[7] For details on the *conscious* awareness, and methods of heightening this conscious awareness, see *Volume 3* in this KEYS TO CONSCIOUSNESS AND SURVIVAL Series, UNVEILING THE HIDDEN INSTINCT.

waves, surface indicators, and other impressions that the deep waters of our minds render.

- We can further recognize, detect, still deeper characteristics of the patterns that affect and inhabit us by developing a sense of the intertwined energy ebbs and flows, streams, entanglements, knots, and other subtle characteristics of patterns.

NAVIGATION SENSING CONCEPT
KNOW YOU HAVE A RIGHT
TO THE USE OF YOUR OWN ENERGY

You can become ever more aware of the *PATTERN TERRAIN* (the *PATTERN TERRAIN* defined in previous chapters of this book), including the **pathways and characteristics of** (textures of) energy flowing through you and through any part of, dimension of, yourself at any moment you choose. Your energy is your *arrangement* of and *allocation* of energy in and out of the patterns and pattern sets you carry.

You help arrange your energy and even store it. You have as much right, if not more right, to the application and use of your energy as anyone or anything else. The energy that patterns consume is not these patterns' energy. This energy belongs to you and others your patterns draw upon and or affect.

Your energy is your energy. Many of your patterns help produce energy for you. Some patterns even distribute, delegate, protect, even save energy for you.

All patterns require energy to operate. Much of the energy your patterns require is your energy; much of your energy and patterns' energy is drawn in from outside you.

Many patterns require your energy to operate. Many *problem* patterns require your energy to operate. These patterns draw upon your energy without necessarily having your conscious permission to do so. Patterns are programmed to take the energy they need, in whatever form they need it, to sustain *themselves*.

Here is the dilemma patterns present. The flow of your energy into patterns that inhabit you takes place largely without you realizing this is happening. Yet, you may or may not wish to provide energy to each of the patterns taking your energy.

You have as much right to your energy as does any pattern that has been formed by you or has overtaken you. What this means is that you have a right to move your energy in and out of patterns that you see as healthiest for yourself (so long as these patterns do no harm to self *or* others).

You also have a right to *remove* your energy from *problem* patterns that are troubling, unhealthy, harmful, and or dangerous.

This is easier said than consciously done.

Those who have struggled to break "bad" habits and or problem patterns (such as drug or nondrug addiction patterns) know how difficult it can be to try to take your energy away from these patterns. Patterns resist you taking your energy away from these patterns. Problem patterns resist quite hard, their sustain functions fight you. They seek to retain use of your energy not for you, but for themselves.

However this pattern's grabbing of your energy for itself has evolved into you, into your programming, this is a powerful function a pattern exhibits.

*A pattern serves itself first,
then perhaps the person or persons it occupies.*

*Nevertheless, problem patterns themselves
should not be allowed to control
the use of, allocation of, arrangement of, your energy.*

You can NAVIGATE, distinguish, yourself and your energy from your problem patterns and from the energy they are drawing from you. Becoming ever more clear about this can be a powerful process…

**Your patterns themselves
consume energy, use this energy,
much of it *your* energy, for themselves.**

**Remember however, <u>you</u> are not your <u>patterns</u>.
Your energy is not property of your patterns per se.**

<u>**NAVIGATION SENSING CONCEPT**</u>
*DETECT A PROBLEM PATTERN THAT IS
USING ENERGY IN PROBLEM WAYS*

We are programmed, by our pattern programming, to allow our energy to naturally go to the patterns inhabiting us. Our patterns will of course "want" this. Patterns are of course programmed, wired, to require energy to work and to remain in place. Our energy can be used "well" (perhaps efficiently, although this is not guaranteed) by a positive, healthy, pattern system. Our energy can be used in harmful ways by an unhealthy pattern system.

While a pattern is simply drawing energy to sustain itself, it may be, without our realizing the extent of this, using this energy in problematic ways such as:

- Generating harm or even great harm while *building, enabling, and or sustaining* that pattern;

- Even hoarding, intensifying, distorting, or draining the energy that pattern holds and uses;

- And or, moving, manipulating, that pattern's energy patterning itself into an out of control mode.

Chapter 28
Deceptive Energy Traps:
Detect Possible,
Emerging, and Actual Situations:
Traps and Paradoxes

Were we some kind of fun electronic game, we might see all this somewhat like a computer game or app. We might visualize what is taking place within and among the patterns we live with and within.

We might see ourselves as players (or pawns) trying to move through a complicated system, perhaps a gaming system. The game might be something about our trying to be well while moving through the system of patterns, or perhaps our trying to survive while moving through the system of problem patterns. We might be trying to protect ourselves, our own SELVES and our own energy, from problem patterns.

We might see complex pattern networks forming, interacting with other pattern networks, competing with each other for control and energy, even competing among themselves for their own agendas.

We would win this game by successfully NAVIGATING these pattern systems.

Similarly, we can ever more consciously *NAVIGATE* the patterns systems that inhabit us, find our way through these networks, and be well, as well as we can be within these systems. Or we can find ways to change or even exit particular patterns within those pattern systems.

NAVIGATION SENSITIZING CONCEPT
SENSITIZE TO PATTERNS'
CONFLICTING ENERGY AGENDAS

Our problem pattern's holding, trapping, and use of our energy for its own purposes produces within us a complex experience. We feel, sense, what is taking place. However, much of what it happening is taking place far beneath our conscious radar.

Certainly some patterns exist to generate and or preserve energy for us. However, many problem patterns use our energy for themselves, require this energy to continue to be the problem patterns that they are.

Problem patterns can cause us to send mixed messages to ourselves. On the one hand, we feel a pattern's requirement for our energy, just as any pattern's requirement for our energy (in the form of the pattern's use of our attention, decision-making, judgement, behavioral responsiveness, etc.). Yet, we may also feel (on some level) the harm the problem pattern is causing us.

Of course, it is entirely natural, even essential, that the healthy patterning we form and live by requires our energy.

Yet, past the level of essential biological operating patterning, and secondary biological patterning supporting this essential patterning, ***our brain does not necessarily*** *manage the distribution of energy to our various pattern systems based on healthy needs for these patterns.* I

n some sense, while our brain is serving as the executive control of us, *the brain is simply allocating energy where patterns call for energy.*

It appears that all too frequently, the brain itself may not fully distinguish a problem pattern as being one less deserving of energy. And, when a pattern becomes a problem pattern, an unhealthy at times even dangerous pattern, it too requires energy. In fact, as the race to dominate our systems appears out of control, problem patterns such as various problem emotional and behavioral pattern addictions arise.

We can be caught in the *mixed agenda* (and mixed energy agenda) posed by our problem patterns. We can feel we are caught, although we may not have distinct words to describe what is actually happening to and within us. We may feel or sense that there are at least two forces or pulls competing, or opposing each other, within us:

> Pull One: Problem patterns are patterns and thus appear to our brain as patterns seeking the energy and attention they require to sustain themselves.

> Pull Two: Yet problem patterns are harming us while they do so.

We feel this *pull-versus-pull* **internal tug of war**, although we may not have an entire understanding of this:

(Pull One)→→→ versus ←←←(Pull Two)

The diagram above, its arrows pointing at each other in a sort of standoff, is a simple picture of a complex situation affecting us. An internal conflicting agenda (what I have described as a *PATTERN WAR*) like this can wreak minor or major havoc upon us.

<u>NAVIGATION SENSITIZING CONCEPT</u>
SENSITIZE TO THE PARADOX OF CONFLICT,
AND TO PARADOXICAL PATTERN TRAPS

We can be caught in this conflicting internal agenda. Sensing what is taking place can help us more consciously *NAVIGATE* our patterns and problem patterns.

We can understand that the simple diagram above pictures an internal mixed agenda, one of competing and conflicting patterns. These arrows pointing toward each other can form a caught, trapped, stuck-stuck, lose-lose sort of situation—a no way out or no comfortable way out situation.

As I explain in depth in BOOK ONE of NAVIGATING LIFE'S STUFF, this is a **PARDOXical pattern trap** locking the energy in a power struggle, a conflict. This conflict is turning the pattern itself against the pattern's host, our SELVES.

Breaking free of this PARDOXical pattern trap is difficult. We find there to be largely unseen forces and factors blocking the way out, blocking the exits, holding the SELF away from the pattern exits.

When we hesitate or even resist shedding a problem pattern, it is important for us to remember that it is the pattern that is resisting.

> *Of course the problem pattern is designed to have us resist shedding that problem pattern....*

SAVE THE HOST vs. SAVE THE PATTERN
CONFLICT / STAND OFF
→ → → vs. ← ← ←

<u>NAVIGATION SENSITIZING CONCEPT</u>
SENSITIZE TO
KEY BASIC CONFLICTS IN OUR PROGRAMMING

Past the basic allocation of energy to support our body's essential operating patterns, other of our patterns do compete for our energy. The more any particular problem pattern or set of problem patterns has woven its way into our identity, the more that problem pattern or set of patterns has made us feel it is part of us. Thus, the harder it is for us (and our brains) to let go of, shed, let die, that problem pattern.

We are programmed to sustain patterns, not necessarily to select on a subconscious level which patterns deserve greater sustaining.

We can think of ourselves as not only *pattern recognition machines* but also *pattern formation machines* (as defined in BOOK ONE of NAVIGATING LIFE'S STUFF). We can see our brains as being in control of allocating energy to both pattern recognition and also pattern formation processes—and then to pattern sustain processes as patterns vie to sustain themselves over other patterns, and also over the will of their hosts (us).

Efficiency in this case is perhaps focused primarily on forming patterns, and then supporting and sustaining patterns that have been formed--*and then coordinating patterns' competition for dominance of the energy available to sustain them, to sustain these patterns.*

In other words, perhaps the brain is a pattern forming and pattern managing utility, rather than an arbiter of which patterns are healthiest.

What this means for us is that we have to be ever more aware that our programming, the programming of our brains, may not be entirely protective of us. Whether this is a glitch in our programming or is a glitch programmed, designed, into us, we cannot know for certain, can we?

Chapter 29
Like Waking Up:
Key Navigation Awareness Concepts

The matter of sensitizing ourselves, fine tuning our awareness, is central although frequently taken rather lightly. This is largely the result of our not being informed regarding how fine tuned we can actually become.

When our own personal awareness is denied or suppressed by our own programming, we want to notice this, to be aware of this.

There are times when
we are being held back from knowing more
by our own programing not to know more.

We can stand up to this programming
by continuously fine tuning
our conscious awareness.

<u>NAVIGATION RESISTANCE AWARENESS</u>
SEE PROBLEM PATTERNS
RESISTING THEIR BEING SHED

The more powerful, the more deeply entrenched, a problem pattern is, the more resistant to change that pattern is. We can become very aware of and alert to the feel of this pattern *resistance* itself.

Of course, many problem emotional and behavioral patterns can be broken or modified. In effect, every change in a pattern is establishing a new pattern.

In this sense, when a pattern is modified, changed, it is moved into being new pattern, thereby shedding parts or all of the old pattern. In this, changing is pattern shedding, at least partial *pattern shedding*.

Whether it be a minor change or a major change of a pattern system or a pattern set, or a cluster of pattern sets, some patterning is being shed, and is therefore undergoing a pattern-dying.

Of course, most everything will resist its own dying. We are programmed to resist dying. At least we do not generally like the idea of our dying. More so, our patterns are programmed to resist their own dying, to therefore do what it takes, use whatever energy of ours it takes, to sustain themselves.

Back to this energy issue: When you are shedding part or all of an existing pattern, you are freeing your energy, the energy that has been locked in by that old pattern system.

Shedding a *problem* pattern system can be challenging in that the *problem* pattern will fight this shedding, will do what it can to remain in place. We can feel this resistance, this fighting, on deep innermost levels of our SELVES.

Those readers who have worked to "break" a problem addiction pattern to alcohol/drugs, or to nondrug behaviors such as gambling, spending, sexing, or to problem emotional patterns, know this. Problem patterns resist our breaking those patterns, work to drag us back into those patterns however they can.

So shedding a pattern faces the effects of that pattern's resistance to its being shed. This does not always feel good, often feels quite unpleasant, even quite bad, as the pattern sends us negative feedback, making us feel that it hurts too much to break that pattern.

NAVIGATION RESISTANCE AWARENESS
FEEL PROBLEM PATTERNS BRING FEAR IN

Do not fear this shedding, this change. The problem pattern employs sensations such as fear to hold you in the problem pattern. While self protective awareness is a powerfully useful sensation, this is not the fear sensation the problem pattern is sending you.

Be aware of the sensation of fear. Examine any fear you may feel. If the fear of breaking a problem pattern arises, know that this is not a healthy fear sensation. This is the opposite. This problem pattern evoked fear congests and weakens your focus.[8] The problem pattern can use this fear to hold you and your energy within it.

Know that the fear of change away from a problem pattern is that pattern's programming of you to help hold this problem pattern in place.

---

[8] I discuss in depth the power of one's focus in personal change in the book, *UNVEILING THE HIDDEN INSTINCT*, which is *Volume 3* in this KEYS TO CONSCIOUSNESS AND SURVIVAL SERIES.

The *problem* pattern programming of course works to have you weak enough to fail to fight the *problem pattern* itself. This means that even you, your *SELF*, have been employed to assist in this pattern's resistance to changing.

Yet, of course change can be all right. Change away from a problem pattern can be, when it is a constructive change in a healthy direction, positive -- despite any sense that such a change does not feel "normal" or "usual" or "good" or "right."

(Note again that: A pattern generally seeks to preserve itself, therefore when we seek to break out of or modify a pattern, even a problem pattern, we feel the pattern itself resisting.)

NAVIGATION RESISTANCE AWARENESS
RECOGNIZE THE
PATTERN'S RESISTANCE TO CHANGE

Change is natural. Remember that there is, throughout the cosmos, a perpetual flow of change, in which forces are *always* interweaving and disentangling, contracting and expanding. Some of this motion is smooth. Some of this motion is rather bumpy, at times rugged, or even convulsive. But all of this is change. Change is incessant.

And so, when a change away from a problem pattern feels in any way like a *crisis or a difficult transition, ending, or death,* understand this as something else: *a movement **into** <u>a new energy arrangement</u>. Change is, after all, the freeing of energy from one set of patterns into the formation of another.*

Moving into a new energy arrangement can feel somewhat like giving birth, or even like dying when the old arrangement resists its being removed or denied control.

NAVIGATION RESISTANCE AWARENESS
UNDERSTAND PARADOX LOCKS

So much energy is held in patterns, locked in patterns. Again note here: All too often, energy is trapped in problem patterns and held there to support these problem patterns, or held there until the energy either drains, degrades, or spins into dangerous states.

When energy is trapped in a pattern, there is a locked-in, no-exit, sort of trapping of that energy, much like the *PARADOXical* energy pattern described in the previous book (*NAVIGATING LIFE'S STUFF: DYNAMICS OF PERSONAL CHANGE. BOOK ONE*). I call this the **PARADOX LOCK** that we can sense present in so many problem pattern sets:

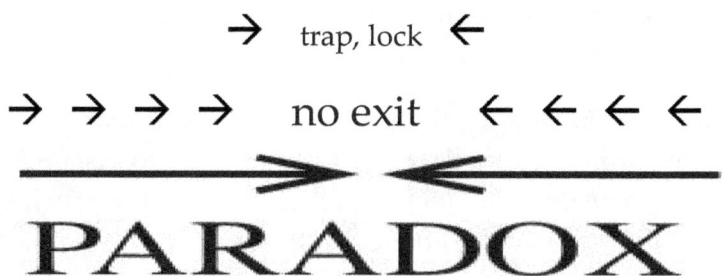

PARADOX Trap, Lock

NAVIGATION RESISTANCE AWARENESS
EVER MORE CLOSELY
DETECT PARADOX LOCKS

We can *fine tune our awareness* to notice when we, our energy, feels stuck or trapped or perhaps otherwise constrained or distorted.

We can fine tune ourselves to sense, **as early as we can**, when we are being drawn into an *energy trapping situation*. We can in this way sense or feel the *PARADOX* here, the pull of the pattern itself to sustain itself, to survive, and the pull of our *SELVES* to help our *SELVES* survive a problem pattern.

All patterns require energy to sustain themselves. Energy is held in patterns, in some cases stuck or trapped in patterns. When energy is trapped in a problem pattern, the problem pattern requires that energy to hold itself, that pattern, in place. Patterns will take the energy, absorb the energy, hold the energy "needed" to maintain their existence/s. Problem patterns can thus become what I have elsewhere defined as problem *energy sinks*.

The energy is held *by* the problem pattern *in* that problem pattern, simply to *enable* the problem pattern to *sustain itself*: *to resist changing, shedding, dying*. Once energy is stuck in a pattern, in a *holding pattern within that pattern*, this is the *PARADOX pattern* or *PARADOXical trap* or *sink*: the *PARADOX lock*, *PARADOXical energy lock*, referred to above and in the previous NAVIGATING LIFE'S STUFF book (BOOK ONE).

Many problem pattern systems interact with, thus are, clusters of overlapping patterns and interweaving pattern sets where *PARADOX* patterns or sub-patterns hold, even hide, themselves trapped within other patterns. These are *PARADOX TRAPS* and *PARADOX LOCKS*. These are in essence, **interacting** *energy traps, sinks, or locks* planted there to sustain the patterns they support.

<u>**NAVIGATION RESISTANCE AWARENESS**</u>
**KNOW ENERGY
TRAPPED IN PATTERNS
MAY RUN AWRY,
RUN WILD, AND OR DETERIORATE**

Some Readers have experienced what is commonly called "burn out." We all know in some way the experience of being caught in a cycle or pattern past the point of choosing to be there for healthy reasons.

Energy held too long, trapped too long, in a pattern may exacerbate, or wobble, or deteriorate. Some problematic patterns do become unbalanced, and intensify, sometimes in quite dangerous ways, when held in place for a long period.

Think of a top spinning out of control, spewing its energy out, and then wobbling, perhaps wobbling dangerously as its loses control of its energy, and then loses it energy.

There are patterns that do indeed deteriorate, at times also in dangerous ways rather than simply "going away." Think about this deterioration.

*When a pattern's energy is trapped, circling, cycling, around and around, closed in on itself, warding off influence from outside itself, from outside its pattern, that pattern's energy is **resisting** outside influence, thus **resisting change**.*

Of course, given that change can cause a pattern to shed, a pattern may resist change to preserve itself.

*This is the **PARADOXical double bind nature of problem patterning**....*

- Resistance to change can lead to *pattern sustaining*, yes. It can also lead to *pattern destabilization* and *pattern stagnation*.
- When a pattern is a problem pattern, this pattern sustaining itself can harm its host, and can harm the healthy patterns the problem pattern has embedded itself within. *PARADOX pattern* upon *PARADOX patterns* emerge within and surrounding these patterns. These *PARADOX patterns* trap the energy.
- A *long term energy trapping PARADOX* can become a danger both by sustaining itself, and or by undergoing destabilization and or a stagnation of its energy.
- Too many elect, of what they believe to be their own Free Will, to resist change away from a problem pattern. Yet, this is the programmed-in patterning that is electing this, not the patterns' host (not us, not you, not ourselves).

- *NAVIGATING* our patterning involves recognizing this reality: ***we are the <u>host/s</u> of the pattern/s, <u>not</u> the pattern/s that have invaded us.***[9]

---

[9] Further explanation of this invasion concept is provided in the book, *SEEING THE HIDDEN FACE OF ADDICTION: DETECTING AND CONFRONTING THIS INVASIVE PRESENCE*. See this and other books listed in the recommended reading section at the end of this present book, *NAVIGATING LIFE'S STUFF: DYNAMICS OR PERSONAL CHANGE, BOOK TWO*.

KEYS TO CONSCIOUSLY MOVING THROUGH OUR PROCESSES AND THEIR PATTERNS

Chapter 30
Dynamics of Personal Change
In Navigating Life's Stuff:
Alerting the Awareness

*We tend not to realize that key in NAVIGATING LIFE'S STUFF are the DYNAMICS OF PERSONAL CHANGE. These dynamics involve key awareness of and sensitivity to the dynamics of **pattern** change.*

Pattern change itself is not always understood as central in our moving through situations and problems we may face. This is not surprising. We have not allowed ourselves or have not been allowed to fully understand what I describe herein, the **dynamics of personal <u>pattern</u> change.**

We are held in an unenlightened state, because we are more easily controlled there—controlled by our own patterns, our own *programming to be trapped in our patterns, forced to play out being caught in, trapped in, feeling dependent upon, addicted to, our patterning itself.*

<u>NAVIGATION ALERT AWARENESS</u>
<u>DETECT PROGRAMMING</u>
<u>TO BE ADDICTED TO PATTERNS</u>

Ever more consciously *NAVIGATING* our *PROCESSES* and *PATTERNS* involves our ever more understanding this about ourselves:

We are programmed to be *addicted* to our patterns. Whether healthy or unhealthy patterns, our programming is designed to hold us within these patterns.

Hence, we are *programmed to become addicted to our patterns*, and then ***addicted to our addictions*** themselves (addicted to our drug, and also to our non-drug emotional and behavioral, even cognitive, *pattern addictions*). The dynamics of personal change I define in this book are about our understanding this about our programming, about our patterns, about our *SELVES*.

NAVIGATION ALERT AWARENESS
UNDERSTAND
CONSCIOUSLY LEAVING A PATTERN

As discussed in previous chapters, key in *NAVIGATING LIFE'S STUFF* is ***consciously shedding*** unhealthy patterns. I have shared this understanding with many clients over many years. Conscious shedding is a key *DYNAMIC OF PERSONAL CHANGE*.

Essential in the process of personal change is <u>consciously</u> leaving or breaking, *shedding*, letting die, patterns of problem behavior, emotion, and thought, whether these be patterns of:

- <u>explicit</u> (obvious visible) problem ***emotional*** patterns and their cycles; and or,

- <u>explicit</u> (obvious, visible) problem ***behavioral*** patterns and their cycles; and or,

- explicit (obvious, visible) problem *substance* (drug/alcohol) use patterns and cycles—and or,

- the still more powerful *implicit* (hidden, largely *invisible*) problem behavioral, emotional, and thought patterns.

NAVIGATION ALERT AWARENESS
UNDERSTAND WE ARE PROGRAMMED

When we think of consciously shedding a pattern, yes, this involves the work many do on themselves while in peer group processes, or therapy processes, or treatment (or even medication) programs. However helpful all this can be, most of this work does not in any way fully address the underlying and basic issue: what it means for us to be ...

programmed
to form and get stuck in patterns.

Consciously shedding problem patterns is a *dynamic process* of *standing up to one's programming itself*. This is about *fine tuning one's awareness* to be ever more sensitized to what it means to be a *highly programmable and programmed being,* one programmed to form and get stuck in patterns, many healthy patterns, and many unhealthy patterns.

Once we realize how programmed to form patterns we are, and once we add to this realization that we are NOT these patterns, we can begin to *separate conceptually from the*

patterns and the pattern programming. We can more fully realize that:

> our programming
> seeks to
> hold us in a state of ignorance regarding,
> to keep us in compliance with,
> to have us even surrender to,
> our programming
> whether or not
> our programming is always healthy for us.

NAVIGATION ALERT AWARENESS
SENSITIZE TO
DEEPLY EMBEDDED
PROGRAMMING TO SUSTAIN PATTERNING

Here again know that problem patterns are not limited to *explicit* emotions and behaviors, or even to what I have defined elsewhere as *explicit* drug/alcohol addiction patterns.[10]

So many other problem patterns affecting us are deeply embedded neural level programmings, some biological level and essential operating patterns, others more surface level yet implicit, less visible, less detectable patterns of thought or emotion or behavior.

---

[10] See my discussion on obvious and less obvious, hidden, addiction patterns in other books I have written such as *TRANSCENDING ADDICTION AND OTHER AFFLICTIONS*, and also *SEEING THE HIDDEN FACE OF ADDICTION: DETECTING AND CONFRONTING THIS INVASIVE PRESENCE*.

As I explain in the previous book, *BOOK ONE* of *NAVIGATING LIFE'S STUFF*: All these patterns are designed to self sustain. In this sense, surface level thought, emotion, and behavior patterns are designed to work as if they are **addictive**. What I elsewhere define as our **addiction function itself** is a powerful **pattern anchor**, a powerful **pattern sustain function**.

Watch for the effects of these pattern sustaining functions – become aware of the details regarding how these affect you.

While many of our patterns are obvious to us, such as in the case of severe alcohol/drug addiction or other nondrug addictions, many of our patterns are operating deeply within us, with their most powerful workings *far out of our conscious awareness.*[11]

Here is where the greatest concern must be. We are frequently dominated by invisible patterns that we cannot see or recognize in full, if at all. These still waters run so very deep and invisibly within us.

How we begin to *sensitize ourselves* to these less visible patterns is key in our *DYNAMIC NAVIGATION OF LIFE'S STUFF*. To begin this self sensitizing, this fine tuning, we must:

- Learn to read ourselves, and our environments, with ever more awareness, and sensitivity.

---

[11] I develop in depth the notion of the <u>**conscious**</u> ***awareness*** in *UNVEILING THE HIDDEN INSTINCT*, which is *Volume 3* in this *KEYS TO CONSCIOUSNESS AND SURVIVAL SERIES*.

- Notice the subtle shifts and variations in our energy, as well as in our attention, our focus.

- Become highly aware of small changes in oneself during the day (and night).

- When subtle shifts in energy levels, attention, focus, etc. are sensed, pay close attention to these. Notice these early, as these arise, as these continue, and where these vary or even recede. See these changes, ebbs and flows, as suggestions and indicators.

- We can consciously decide to, and then begin to detect, the presence of patterns, and of the underlying core patterns, and of even deeper underlying programming driving these patterns.

- We can begin to sense that we are being occupied by, invaded by, patterns—and that these patterns are NOT us, not our SELVES although allowing us to confuse ourselves with them.

NAVIGATION ALERT AWARENESS
SEE THAT PATTERN SHEDDINGS
CAN BE PARTIAL
OR MORE COMPLETE

Sheddings of patterns can be partial or perhaps also more complete (when and where full shedding of a pattern or pattern system is at all possible). Generally, pattern clusters are more complex and thus more difficult to shed all at once. Patterns embed, disguise, and entangle themselves.

Problem patterns, being in essence just patterns, embed themselves in patterns that are healthy, essential, or in some other way somewhat necessary for us. Problem patterns embed themselves in healthy, even essential patterns, *to operate on deep even deceptively essential levels.* (See the related definition of the Trojan Horse effect I offer in SEEING THE HIDDEN FACE OF ADDICTION: DETECTING AND CONFRONTING THIS INVASIVE PRESENCE.)

Problem patterns, like still (seemingly still) waters, run deep. We may see evidence of these patterns. Yet, these bits of evidence are tips of the icebergs.

Hence, quite often we see efforts to change being focused on stopping, shedding, letting die, just a visible <u>part</u> of a problem behavior pattern rather than an entire pattern set or cluster. (Of course, shedding everything clustered with a problem pattern might be virtually impossible, or cause physical death. Other strategies for personal awareness and NAVIGATION provide more realistic and powerful attention to these patterns.)

Especially when the set or cluster of patterns includes deeply embedded, highly implicit, very difficult to detect anywhere close to in full, patterning, shedding patterns is an *intensive, highly sensitive and sensitized process* requiring that we:

turn on our sensors
even at the
micro level of our SELVES and our awareness.

Certainly, we can respond by asking ourselves: *what and how can we deal with what we do not know (do not consciously know) is there?* To start, we can awaken our awareness to the various approaches and keys to *NAVIGATION* offered in this book.

Chapter 31
Deepening Our Reading
Of The Pattern Network

There are infinite levels of the DYNAMICS OF PERSONAL CHANGE being described in these NAVIGATING LIFE'S STUFF books. Much of this particular volume (BOOK TWO) seeks to heighten our awareness of the subtle, less visible, inner workings of patterns and pattern programming upon us.

In this chapter, the discussion regarding alerting our awareness is continued, here talking about our deepening our reading of the pattern and patterning networks we move through as we live.

NAVIGATION SENSATION ALERT
ALERT TO FAR DEEPER
SENSATIONS AND SENSITIVITIES

We can also activate, turn on, our deeper alert sensitivities by noting:

(1) There will always be the continuing issue of how to change a single problem pattern when it is tied into a whole pattern set or cluster. (For example, how to stop addictively using a particular drug when that drug using behavior is tied into complex webs, patterns, of family, social, financial, emotional, nutritional, and other conditions and behaviors--as well as uses of other drug and or nondrug addictive behaviors).

(2) There is also the largely unrecognized issue of the powerful yet implicit, unseen, subconscious and unconscious (what I elsewhere describe as *highly subliminal*) *patterning and programming* levels of emotional, psychological, as well as nutritional, biochemical, neurotransmitter, brain chemistry, etc. patterning.

This is the underlying patterning generating and supporting any explicit emotional and or behavioral problem pattern.

(Here is a somewhat obvious example: A person exhibiting severe self harm habits such as self cutting may be responding to underlying trauma, such as vague memories of traumatic experiences, when self-harming on a regular basis. Addressing the self harm habit without yet sensing, seeing, and consciously recognizing, the *power of the pattern cluster in which that habit is enmeshed* is not going to be enough to fully detect and then shed that harm pattern.)

(3) Of course, treatment professionals will respond by saying they do know the above two points, that they do "treat the whole person."

Certainly, this can be the intention of various comprehensive and holistic approaches, and also of particular "cognitive" and other approaches.[12]

---

[12] This is not to criticize CBT and DBT and other cognitive approaches, rather to suggest that there is also a still deeper level of our functioning to be aware of, focused on: This is our programming to be patterned. (See

Yet, actually being highly, purposefully, aware of the nature and power of *patterning itself, and the power of the programming we all carry to instate and retain our patterns*, is not itself an explicit part of the treatment being provided or the theory driving that treatment.

(4) *NAVIGATING LIFE'S STUFF* makes the concepts offered in this book central in all work and teaching done with ourselves and others.

Here, KEYS TO NAVIGATING OUR PROCESSES AND PATTERNS are offered and made front and center as these offer the power of seeing meaning in, and the truth about, our processes and their patterns.

(5) We can and must learn and practice the awarenesses I describe in these *NAVIGATING LIFE'S STUFF* books. These are in essence the keys themselves, the keys to sensing, seeing, detecting, understanding, moving through, NAVIGATING, the processes and patterns we experience.

These are actually also the processes and patterns contained within and surrounding our experiences (such as experiences of life challenges, changes, transitions, endings, and deaths).

---

the detailed footnote on the history of "cognitive behavioral" approaches at the end of *Chapter 1* of the previous book, *BOOK ONE* of *NAVIGATING LIFE'S STUFF*.)

NAVIGATION SENSATION ALERT
SENSITIZE TO
CHANGING AND SHEDDING OPPORTUNITIES

Some sheddings are complete cut-offs, endings, abrupt deaths of *patternings*.

Some sheddings can have powerfully positive outcomes in that these sheddings of problem patterns can lead to profound transitions, transformations, and transcendences of those patterns.

Imagine a snake shedding its skin. Although we cannot know what the snake experiences, we can imagine such a change in ourselves, what the intense process can be like. Change is frequently quite intense.

<u>Patterns resist change</u> *via their deeply embedded sustain functions. Shedding the skin is shedding patterning which can be quite profound.*

People *can* change.

Yes, the change may be registering or appear to be registering in the people themselves. *Yet the change is taking place in the patterns people form and follow,*[13] *the*

---

[13] Various research regarding brain and behavior change indicates neuronal activity in numerous behavior change related realms, including but not limited to that triggering metabolic changes in specific processes such as brain protein metabolism. While new motor behaviors concurrent with changes in brain level processes have been recorded, emotional and other less physically apparent changes, while also having been measured, raise questions regarding the longevity of the changes, their durability,

patterns OCCUPYING, INHABITING, their minds and bodies, living within what they may feel, may be programmed to feel, is their own Free Will.

When people die physical deaths, they shed their physical bodies. Basically, most of our physical deaths take place when we have grown terminally ill, or have outgrown, worn out, over-damaged, or simply outlived, our bodies.

We then shed our physical bodies. Our bodies are then no longer the physical vehicles we travel in. (Refer again to the previous book, NAVIGATING LIFE'S STUFF: DYNAMICS OF PERSONAL CHANGE: BOOK ONE: the chapter titled, *Meet Your Vehicle,* and also the *Appendices* of that book.)

The same is true of our relationships, our jobs, our addictions, and any of our behaviors. These are actually patterns and pattern systems ruling us, our *SELVES,* our thoughts, our emotions, and our behaviors.

**NAVIGATION SENSATION ALERT
KNOW WHEN YOUR SKIN'S TOO TIGHT**

Yes, too often the pressure to shed sneaks up on us. We finally notice that the skin of a relationship, a behavior, a phase of life, is far too tight—that we have *outgrown it the way a snake outgrows its skin.*

---

and or the level of learning these changes actually incur. For discussion of levels of learning, see chapters on learning in GESTALTING ADDICTION: SPEAKING TRUTH TO THE POWER AND DEFINITION OF ADDICTION, ADDICTION THEORY, AND ADDICTION TREATMENT.

.

You can get more out of the shedding process by recognizing when you are at its *threshold*.

Become ever more aware of your patterns, even of ***your position in your pattern processes.*** How do you do this? Become highly alert to subtle indications:

- Notice when, to what degree, and how you may be feeling anxious, claustrophobic, and or trapped — physically, emotionally, intellectually, spiritually.

- Notice when, to what degree, and how you may at times or even regularly be exhibiting troubled behavior (behavior which is detrimental to yourself and or others).

- Notice when, to what degree, and how you may be feeling you function on automatic — mindlessly.

- Notice when, to what degree, and how you may experience shifts in your ability to concentrate.

- Notice when, to what degree, and how you may experience changes in your enthusiasm.

- Notice when, to what degree, and how you may respond when you stop for a moment's reflection and ask yourself, "Who am I and why am I here?"

- Notice when, to what degree, and how you may feel or find that your (even daily) life takes on less and less meaning for you — pay attention.

When you become alert to the above:

- Be aware of these sensations.

- Observe these sensations, even the subtle sensations you sense.

Ask yourself:

- What are the patterns that are inhabiting you, the patterns that seek to remain in place, telling you what you must do and feel and think?

- How are these patterns telling you to notice, or minimize, or ignore, or even deny your sensations regarding these patterns?

- What are *you* telling *yourself* to do and feel and think? Does this differ or even conflict with what the patterns are telling you? CAN YOU SENSE THE DIFFERENCE?

NAVIGATION SENSATION ALERT
BE IN TOUCH WITH
DEEP SURVIVAL MESSAGES

Be ever more aware of the hidden and subtle aspects of what is happening within you. What are you telling yourself? What can you hear from deep within *YOU*, from within your *SELF* there behind all those emotional and behavioral patterns you live with? (***Can you hear your SELF? And, how can you know that what you hear is your SELF and not your programming to believe your SELF is your programming?***)

Survival becomes a central yet elusive matter deep within our minds. *So much of what we know and sense is information we are not aware we are knowing and sensing.* We must be ever more aware of what our problem pattern programming is doing to us, and is directing within us.

**We must grow ever more adept at
consciously detecting our
mental, emotional, biological terrain,
even the
PATTERN TERRAIN itself.**

****

Do not assume that only physical survival has meaning. Physical survival, while of course clearly essential, will have different meanings to every one of us, in different times and parts of our lives.[14]

Ask: Is what I am experiencing some form of *STRUGGLE pattern*? Does this feel like the push pull of a *STRUGGLE pattern* even if I cannot define the exact details of the *STRUGGLE*?

---

[14] See other books in this *KEYS TO CONSCIOUSNESS AND SURVIVAL SERIES* where I delve further into matters such as: How we relate to our survival now and perhaps even after we "survive," depending upon the effect of achieving this survival on the consciousness or self or soul. See *Volume 4* in this series, *HOW TO DIE AND SURVIVE*.

Is this a STRUGGLE for your survival __or__ for the survival of your problem pattern/s? Is this you __or__ your problem pattern/s seeking to survive? [15]

Your problem patterns can more easily control you, the host, when you do what you are guided, forced, compelled, to do by your *deceptive problem patterns* (which have invaded you). When you find these problem patterns directing you to do what it takes to survive, continue to ask: what is it that these patterns seek to have survive? You __or__ your problem patterns themselves?

NAVIGATION SENSATION ALERT
KNOW IF AND WHEN TO GET OUT

You know when it is time to shed your "skin" (your patterns). You are caged in, boxed in, trapped, by the patterns of your life; you are losing your *SELF* and your Free Will. Can you separate your problem patterns from your healthy patterns? Can you let your problem patterns die before they kill you or at least kill or harm your Will? Can you let your problem patterns die so that you can survive?[16]

Once you allow yourself to see the truth, you will more and more feel this truth: *You are not your patterns.*

---

[15] See *BOOK ONE* of *NAVIGATING LIFE'S STUFF* where the idea of the underlying *STRUGGLE pattern* so present in so many problem pattern systems is defined.

[16] See also other books in this *KEYS TO CONSCIOUSNESS AND SURVIVAL Series*, such as *HOW TO DIE AND SURVIVE* and also *UNVEILING THE HIDDEN INSTINCT*.

You do not need to stay stuck, trapped, in problem patterns (no matter how much the problem patterns demand you stay stuck in them). You can be ever more alert to the presence and nature of your patterns in order to see, to detect, the need for shedding these problem patterns.

Letting your patterns work themselves so deeply into you that you feel you must maintain your patterns or die, is a false choice. This is <u>not</u> you choosing between you and yourSELF. This is you choosing between you and your patterns, even your problem patterns which seek to dominate you, seek to have you feel these patterns <u>are</u> you.

Once you see this, you can begin to let yourself out of the lie your problem patterns are telling you — let yourself out of your (your patterns') skin which is your pattern system matrix (which is generally camouflaging itself as your *SELF*.

This is where there is sometimes quite a strong resistance: Either you or the people around you (*their* patterns), OR <u>YOUR</u> PATTERNS THEMSELVES, do not want you to change, do not really want you to let go of the patterns that control your behavior, your decision making, your attention, and your other functions and behaviors.

Take conscious steps to *NAVIGATE* the shedding, the death, of your problem pattern/s, of the body of behavior you have outgrown and or must outgrow.

*Open your eyes to the opportunities for exit from pattern traps, see the **exit opportunities** (for example, the energetic forks and*

windows) open to you. These are everywhere. (See the following chapters.)

Do not let anyone tell you that you cannot get there from here. This statement reveals our deep programming to believe in severe limitations. You *can* move out of problem patterns. You can do this as you ever more consciously NAVIGATE your life journey.

PART NINE

KEYS IN
NAVIGATING THE INTENSITY

Chapter 32
Empowering Navigation Elements

These are the basic *NAVIGATIONAL approaches* listed at the opening of BOOK ONE of NAVIGATING LIFE'S STUFF:

- *Understanding* what a pattern or pattern system, and a pattern set, and a pattern cluster, is.
- *Knowing* the basic characteristics of our patterns, pattern systems, so we can better know what we are experiencing.
- *Mapping* our movement into and within the patterns, pattern systems, we form.
- *Recognizing* the characteristics of the processes *and the patterns dictating our processes* that we form in our journeys.
- *Seeing* where we can get caught in patterns, in repeat patterns, and which of these may be problem patterns or interact with problem patterns.
- *Sensitizing* ourselves to our opportunities for choices among, exits from, and changes (adaptations) in, the processes and patterns we live by and within.
- *Moving through* our PATTERN TERRAINS, our patterns and or pattern systems, pattern sets, and pattern clusters, by consciously sensing the presence of, characteristics of, and opportunities for exit from, patterns we may wish to leave.

Sensitizing ourselves to our movement into, through, and when needed *out*, of our patterns gains us ever more say in how we *experience* our lives. It is essential we recognize the importance of being able to *spot places and times in our processes and patterns* where we can shift, amend (adapt), and ever more adeptly NAVIGATE our energy patterns and our SELVES *through* our PATTERN TERRAINS, our energy patterns, pattern systems, and their programming.

NAVIGATION EMPOWERING ELEMENT
UNDERSTAND
HEALTHY PATTERN CHARACTERISTICS

The notion of healthy pattern characteristics is a tricky concept …. There are hidden truths that must be said here. So, before moving on with this NAVIGATIONAL ELEMENT, let's reveal the truth about what patterns are up to:

1) When we are fine tuning ourselves to see what situations (and their patterns) are healthy for us, we are also fine tuning our awareness of what may not be healthy for us. Once we sense this, we can select a route. Do we amend the pattern we are in? Or do we leave the pattern we are in?

2) **Defining for ourselves what a healthy pattern feels like or looks like is valuable. Patterns are in themselves systems, arrangements of energy, and also elements and movements of energy into and through these arrangements. In this sense, we can look at what forms a healthy system of patterns.**

3) While *systems theory* itself has detailed characteristics of healthy systems, here let us simply consider a few aspects of healthy systems in terms of patterns themselves being systems,

whether micro-level systems or large scale macro-level systems:

4) For a system, which is actually a *pattern system*, to sustain itself, to continue its existence, it must continue at least these functions:

   (a) Continue the flow of energy into itself, into this pattern system, as this energy supplies this pattern system with its primary resource, this energy. An alternative option to this is (b) immediately below....
   (b) Trap and then hold and preserve the energy required by this pattern system to maintain itself, not allowing this energy to leak away or be taken away by other systems or purposes.
   (c) Maintain the flow of the energy this pattern system takes in, continue the energy flow throughout itself, throughout this pattern system, thereby supporting and fueling itself to continue existing.
   (d) Utilize this energy in ways that are (for this pattern system itself) self-sustaining ways.
   (e) Have functions in place that protect this pattern system, functions that keep the system or enemies of this system from misplacing or mis-utilizing this pattern system's energy in ways that deplete or harm this pattern.
   (f) Protect itself, protect this pattern system, from destabilization of itself.

(g) Protect itself, protect this pattern system from depletion of itself.
(h) Avoid other encroaching pattern systems from usurping or invading this pattern system.
(i) Maintain boundaries that protect this pattern system in the face of encroachment, invasion, depletion.

Keep in mind that a healthy pattern system is one that sustains and maintains *itself*.

THIS IN NO WAY SAYS THAT THIS PATTERN SYSTEM IS FOREVER AND ALWAYS HEALTHY FOR THE PERSON OR PLACE IT INHABITS.

A healthy pattern (pattern system) seeks to do what sustains *itself*, which may or may not sustain the host in the long run. This is of course essential and positive for all our essential and positive pattern systems.

Yet, these same healthy system characteristics listed on the previous page are invoked in *problem* pattern self-sustain processes. For example, many dangerous addictions are extremely unhealthy for their hosts, for *us*, yet are healthy pattern systems in that they are succeeding in surviving for quite some time as the patterns, the pattern systems, they are.

NAVIGATION EMPOWERING ELEMENT
DIFFERENTIATE BETWEEN
HEALTHY PATTERN CHARACTERISTICS
AND WHAT IS
HEALTHY FOR THE HOST OF THE PATTERN

Once we understand what allows a pattern system to be healthy, it is essential we understand that a pattern that <u>is</u> effective in maintaining and sustaining <u>itself</u> IS NOT NECESSARILY A HEALTHY PATTERN FOR ITS HOST. While this is quite obvious, we who are pattern hosts may not realize in full the importance of this pattern system awareness. We are programmed not to know, not to sense, this.

This realization is a difficult one to achieve. Certainly, many Readers will note here that problem patterns such as self harming addictions tend to cause their hosts (who suffer these problem patterns) negative feedback from these patterns themselves (such as withdrawal or craving symptoms) -- *when the hosts consider leaving those problem patterns.*

Here again is the key point: *It is NOT THE HOST resisting, it is the PATTERN THAT IS RESISTING our moving out of this pattern.*

We must work to *differentiate ourselves* from our patternings, to know that *our* purpose is to sustain our SELVES, not the patterns that inhabit us.

We must also know that a key function of patterns themselves is the ***pattern sustain function*** I have defined more fully in the preceding book, BOOK ONE of NAVIGATING LIFE'S STUFF.

This *sustain function* is about preserving the pattern no matter what it does to its host, even if the pattern eventually harms the host. We see this in (the tip of the iceberg) explicit addiction patterns such as drug, gambling, spending, and other addictions. We must also look to see this in less explicit, less visible patterns, far below the visible tip of the iceberg so to speak, working deep within us and our programming.

Keep in mind that patterning is programming to continue within, repeat, even stay trapped in, an attitude, emotion, and or behavior. We are indeed creatures who are programmed to be programmable. And the programming that runs us uses patterning to do so.

Chapter 33
Essential
Navigation Keys, I

In my work over many years helping several thousand people move through their lives, I have found there to be what I describe as **key indicators of, and opportunities for, personal fortification and change.**

These are **dynamic opportunities for personal adaptation and change,** *opportunities for energetic sensation, sensitized decision, and highly attuned action.*

When I refer to **opportunities** *here, I am speaking of openings to increasing awareness of what I describe as the* **patterning environment and PATTERN TERRAIN** *we are always moving through, and areas of our SELVES doing this moving through.*

<u>NAVIGATION KEY</u>
SENSITIZE TO KEY PATTERN SHIFTING
(AMENDING, ADAPTING) OPPORTUNITIES

Clearly, we can consciously and markedly increase our awareness of the less visible aspects of ourselves and our patterns to have more say in our experience of living.

We can define for ourselves what *areas of SELF* mean to us, and what these *areas of SELF* feel to us to be. Imagine that you are moving through that seaweed bed referred to in BOOK ONE of NAVIGATING LIFE'S STUFF. That description suggested that moving through the PATTERN TERRAIN, our patterning and its programming, is like moving through a seaweed bed. This web, network, of neural pathways and directives is dense, and although invisible to us in our daily lives, quite dominating of us.

Now imagine that the seaweed and its tangled tendrils are energy streams, arrangements, patterns, invisible strings interweaving to form patterns and to hold these patterns in place.

Now imagine that this seaweed bed of invisible patterns is something best seen with our eyes closed, so that we are **hyperaware** *of the nature of what I describe as* **the PATTERN TERRAIN, the pattern environment** *we are moving through.*

Close your eyes a moment. Put your hands out and imagine you can feel, sense, the tangle, the matrix, of patterns surrounding you. Imagine, visualize, the texture of this pattern environment.

Imagine, or sense, feel, where there are areas of light moving through these energy patterns, where these patterns are less dense, lighter in nature.

Feel also where there are areas of dense, more entangled patternings, where these energy or pattern tendrils are heavily intertwined and quite difficult to see or feel or move through.

Imagine you move your hands through this pattern environment and feel/see places where you can feel/sense/find your way out, places where you can even rearrange the pattern or patterns you sense are present.

Begin to sense places where there is information you can use to move through or even leave this energy patterning, this seaweed bed-like <u>energy pattern environment or PATTERN TERRAIN</u>.

NAVIGATION KEY
BE AWARE OF NAVIGATIONAL ELEMENTS

Fine tuning the awareness to sensitize ourselves to *systems and system levels* is key in moving through the pattern environment within and around ourselves, the milieu in which we live.

We can sensitize to key NAVIGATIONAL ELEMENTS by defining these, knowing what a NAGIVATIONAL ELEMENT can be. We can alert ourselves to these elements as these appear. Each of us will develop many NAVIGATIONAL KEYS of our own. The following are just some essential keys....

As a way of life, part of living in our bodies and minds, we can add ever increasing, always fine-tuning, sensory, emotional, perceptual awarenesses to our list of what we already see and know. This is not about increasing a level of fear or paranoia in our lives, rather this is about being able to detect and understand the realities we live in and move through.

NAVIGATION KEY
SPOT WINDOWS OF OPPORTUNITY

This is about *choosing to be alert* to subtleties. This is about feeling variations and shifts in the *texture of the pattern*

environment we live in and move through, the PATTERN TERRAIN. **This is about choosing to continuously be sensitive to openings,** *windows of opportunity.* **This is about how this sensitization of ourselves can become a part of our living process, can be instilled in our way of being.**

This is not to say that we are or must be seeking a way out of every pattern (situation) we find ourselves in. Of course not. We live within and among many positive and even essential patterns and patternings. We are programmed to be able to live based on our patternings.

This is to say that it is best we are always able to check in with ourselves, and with the energy environments we are in or moving through, to be sure we are not at some point soon, or perhaps much later if at all, going to be stuck or trapped in a pattern that is not healthy for us.

Consider your own experiences with this issue. Have there been times when you were vaguely aware, or perhaps aware in some way but not fully, that you were seeing signs a pattern system you were living in or with was not healthy for you?

What did you do with those signs, those indications that the pattern was not good for you? How did you either ignore, or address in some way yet perhaps not fully, these indicators?

If you were in a similar situation again, what indicators would you consider significant, important to pay attention to?

> LIST AND REMEMBER THESE INDICATORS
> AS YOU NAVIGATE YOUR LIFE.

NAVIGATION KEY
SENSE OPENINGS,
EXIT DOORS, SAFE PASSAGES

You can begin to sensitize to your *pattern environment*. You can grow ever more aware of the unseen yet (once looking closely) quite apparent pattern networks that inhabit you and that you inhabit.

You can begin to sense, or see in your mind's eye, the flow, streams, and moving grids, full of tendrils, lines, vectors, knots, elements of patternings moving throughout you and surrounding you. As you do, you can become aware of yourself traveling, moving around, within, and through this *PATTERN TERRAIN*, this *pattern environment*. This awareness is itself a powerful NAVIGATIONAL KEY.

As you *move through* this *pattern environment*, which you are always doing, notice, sense, imagine if you wish to, areas of the pattern environment that are less dense, less enmeshed in their own patternings. Also notice areas that are more dense, more enmeshed in their own patternings.

Also begin to sensitize to the reality that patterns vary in nature. Some patterns do carry quite strong and very deeply embedded self sustain functions. And some of these powerful patterns are problem patterns. It is important to develop *PATTERN NAVIGATION SKILLS* as these are key in moving through patterns, even in dealing with, even at times surviving, problem patterns.

See or sense or imagine places in the pattern environment where you sense you move more freely, being less restrained or constrained (or held back or weighed down) by the energetic density of patterns controlling your direction, your will, your energy.

These less dense places you sense you can more easily move through are *potential openings, possible doorways* **to pathways and passages through, perhaps even out of, areas of this** *PATTERN TERRAIN*—**should you wish to move out of, to exit, these.**

Sensitize yourself to differences in perceived density, sensed entanglement, so you teach yourself to be aware, even on a non-verbal level, of the characteristics of the patternings that operate you and even occupy you.

Sense, with your intuition or imagination or visualization skills, areas in this pattern environment where you may move most freely, least restricted by or controlled by patterns and their tendrils, arms, vectors.

Keep these freer areas, these openings, in mind. Get to know what these feel like.

You may at some time want to find again, or sense again, these openings, as you may want to move through these openings into passages, in to places you can most easily move through, and perhaps even beyond. These openings are important characteristics of the pattern system terrain.

Mark these openings in your mind, as these are potential entries <u>***into potentially safe passages into personal adaptation and change***</u>.

You can give these openings markers, symbols, or imaginary icons, mental street signs--so you can more readily see these the next time you wish to or need to.

NAVIGATION KEY
LEARN EXIT AND DETOUR OPTIONS

Also as you move through your **PATTERN TERRAIN**, recall any openings (or possible openings) to potential safe passages you may have previously detected.

These exit doors may not be clearly labelled, as exit doors in buildings usually are. However, if you are looking closely, you will be able to sense these signs. Pay attention to sensations saying *EXIT HERE*. Look closely at these *EXIT OPTIONS*. Are these what they say they are?

Keep your eye on what you are being told about where to go, on where you are being pulled to or into. *Always be aware of the pulls you feel. These are patterns pulling.* Many of these pulls are legitimate and healthy for you. Some are not. So again, always look closely at the pulls you feel. This will help you detect and evaluate new openings, especially and ideally, openings to safe passages and their safe patterns.

You will come upon many opportunities for partial or full pattern exit, and or opportunities to detour a particular passage area within a pattern or problem pattern.

Some of these openings may be clear to you and may most clearly appear to be exits to safe passages. Other of these may be less clear and only seem to be to exits to safe passages. Other of these openings will clearly not be exits to safe passages.

Other of these openings may be *detours*: These may be to shorter or safer or clearer ways of moving through this PATTERN TERRAIN with less drag on you, with fewer pattern tendrils holding you back.

Examine your response to the openings, exits, and detours, you come upon. Notice your response to these openings. Listen to your SELF regarding these opportunities, these openings. What do you hear your SELF, not "your" patterns, but your SELF, telling you?

Understand that your awareness of the nature of these **energy or opportunity openings** will evolve and grow more sensitized as you practice being highly alert.

A word about alternatives, pattern detours. Frequently, when we are caught in a *pattern challenge* or *pattern trap*, we miss detecting alternatives. These alternatives are not always simply and clearly safe passages; sometimes these alternatives are in the form of detours.

Get to know, generate awareness of within your own imagination, how a detour feels, how a detour appears. Sense how detours are *adaptations in your journey through the* PATTERN TERRAIN.

Also, be alert to the possibility that you can at times be perceiving false detours, means of capturing your awareness to hold you within the pattern you are seeking to detour or leave. The pattern you are moving through may seek to prevent your exiting it, or your detouring it, to avoid, circumvent, it (or its control over you).

Chapter 34
Essential
Navigation Keys, II

We are constantly moving within and through patterns, pattern sets and pattern clusters, minor and major pattern systems and networks. Finding our way through is only part of the challenge. Knowing where we are and what we are swimming in, and how not to get lost there, is also essential.

NAVIGATION KEY
SPOT ENERGY VARIATIONS, SHIFTS

As you exist within, even move through while within, this **patterning terrain**, be aware of the marked **variations in density**, in energy.

Detect change in the energy texture and its terrain. Sense that your conscious and targeted awareness of the patterns and PATTERN TERRAIN you are dealing with **can fine tune itself, becoming ever more sensitized to otherwise unseen, unnoticed, aspects of the patterning reality you are within.**

There is so much advice available to people dealing with patterns they wish to amend or leave, and this is useful advice. There are even many treatment programs, even medications, addressing people's need for help with problem drug/alcohol use and other difficult emotional and behavioral patterns.

(IMPORTANT NOTE: Reader, again note that if you feel this is you who are in need of treatment or medication, or otherwise needing help with problem patterns, see a health professional immediately. This book is no substitute for professional diagnosis, health care, or treatment.)

However much advice and assistance is offered to treat or help with problem emotional and behavioral patterns, the very important yet very unseen, subtle, aspects of the pattern system, pattern environment, *PATTERN TERRAIN*, are not talked about, all too often not even acknowledged or recognized in any explicit way.

Pattern systems are programmed (structured) not to reveal aspects of themselves that may work against their own sustain functions. This makes sense from the pattern's standpoint. The pattern seeks to sustain itself, therefore seeks to hide its weaknesses.

Yes, it makes sense that patterns do not "want" their full nature recognized by their hosts (or for that matter by those treating explicit problem patterns).

Note that using the term "want" here does not say these patterns have wills of their own. Programming to proceed with an agenda, a *pattern agenda*, does not necessarily give that pattern itself personality or Free Will, or a Will of some sort. However, a *pattern agenda*, a *pattern purpose*, exists. (I discuss the character of patterns in greater depth in other books.) Here, the point is that patterns are designed, are programmed, to sustain themselves as patterns, for the sake of their patterns.

It is essential we allow ourselves to sense, in what ever manner we can, our *patterning sensations themselves*. We can fine tune our focus, fine tune our awareness, to intuitively sense ever more. Be aware, it is a good idea. **We can begin to allow ourselves to detect generally undefined and thus generally unmarked areas of these patterns, their patterning passages, their patterning terrains.**

What we can begin to sense is what we may be programmed not to fully sense. When we do not sense what is taking place, our patternings are protecting, sustaining themselves by *working on us so deeply under our own radar.* This allows many of the most insidious aspects of the most invasive problem patterning to remain unseen, unnoticed, not recognized, not defined as important or even as existing.

Here is where our ever increased sensitivity to patterning effects is essential, as here is where we can ever more consciously detect, confront, NAVIGATE, our patterns and their passages.[17]

Hold your hands out in front of you, or imagine that you are doing so. Think of your hands, your palms, or the ideas of your hands and palms, as sensors, antennae-like readers of the environment, reading the unseen yet very present environment you are in. Let

---

[17] Refer to the discussion of the Trojan Horse concept in the book, *SEEING THE HIDDEN FACE OF ADDICTION: DETECTING AND CONFRONTING THIS INVASIVE PRESENCE.*

your sensors read the energy terrain around and within you. Where are the pattern presences you can feel, almost see? Where are these pattern presences enmeshing you so thoroughly that you may have to work hard to break free if you choose to?

Think about the notion of BEING ENMESHED. When you are swimming through that entangled bed of seaweed referred to earlier, that PATTERN TERRAIN, you may become entangled in it. You may be caught, even trapped in it. Your energy may be entangled, enmeshed, and drawn away from you.

When the bed of seaweed is the pattern system inhabiting YOU, you become enmeshed in what appears to be yourself. However, you are not the patterns and pattern systems that inhabit you. There is a SELF somewhere amidst it all. This is YOU. Keep the SELF, your SELF, in mind as you NAVIGATE the patterns that inhabit you.

NAVIGATION KEY
NOTE PASSAGE AND PATTERN DISTURBANCES AND IRREGULARITIES

As you sense, as you apply your sensors to reading, your environment, imagine you are able to sense, detect, energy disturbances and irregularities. What do these mean to you? How do you read these? When do you become aware of these? How do you know when you are becoming aware?

Can you begin to detect pattern characteristics that are so subtle, so vague, so hidden, that these are difficult to describe in words? **You know these are there, you can feel their presence, yet little language has been devoted to describing** *the unseen PATTERN TERRAIN occupying us. So we must open our inner eye.*

This drive to detect pattern characteristics is valuable when it calls attention to energy disturbances and implicit pattern addictions that might not otherwise be seen.

Sometimes we detect pattern characteristics once these become explicit, more obvious in some way. We thus wait until there is a physical problem we can see, we can hang our hat on so to speak, to address it.

This is frequently the case with physical issues and behaviors. While this is quite useful in identifying the hidden presence of an underlying problem pattern, this is not where we want to first become aware of problem patterning.

The making explicit, the physicalizing or somatizing of a hidden condition can result in physical suffering without any healing or even any clear recognition of the condition from which it stems.

Basically, you can make yourself sick pulling the energy in to physical form to draw your attention to yourself, unless you are trained to work with it. (Again, if you feel this is happening to you, see a health treatment professional right away.)

<u>**NAVIGATION KEY**</u>
KNOW WARNING SIGNS

Most Readers have traveled actual on-ground roads and highways where signs marking road hazards, falling boulders, roadwork, etc., are present. We can be grateful much of these are marked for us.

What are not well marked (if marked at all) for us are hazard signs or alerts we may want as we move through the *invisible PATTERN TERRAIN of our lives*. These signs and alerts are not readily available or easy to detect, if present. We nevertheless do best to want to see these, read these, detect these, to become aware of these as these arise—or should arise if not being prevented from coming to our attention.

NAVIGATION KEY
DETECT ENERGY TRAPS

One of the key signs we want to be able to detect, to read, along our way is any sign that we face or are passing or confronting, what I describe herein (and more fully in *BOOK ONE*) as being an *energy trap*.

What is an **energy trap**? Imagine you have been lost in your life, caught in a situation you see no ready, no easy, way out of, if any way at all.

Perhaps this feels to you to be a no exit, no win, sort of stuck situation defined earlier as an energy trap (defined as a *PARADOXical energy trap* and described in depth in *BOOK ONE* of *NAVIGATING LIFE'S STUFF: DYNAMICS OF PERSONAL CHANGE*.) Imagine a time when you were faced with a seeming no way out, or no easy way out, situation or pattern.

See again the *PARADOX* figure diagrammed in *BOOK ONE*:

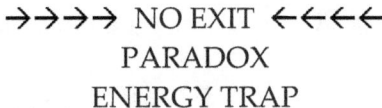

→→→→ NO EXIT ←←←←
PARADOX
ENERGY TRAP

We can find ourselves caught in such a situation without seeing how we have arrived there. Imagine for a moment you are caught in such a situation. Ask yourself: what does this feel like? How do I know this is what is going on? How did I get here? What were the early signs I was heading into this trap? Is this a no-exit trap, or other difficult situation, I can indeed NAVIGATE? **YES.**

When energy is caught, trapped in such a PARADOX, that energy is not available to us. That energy is being utilized to sustain the PARADOX pattern itself.

NAVIGATION KEY
SEE, SENSE, DETECT FORKS IN OUR ROADS

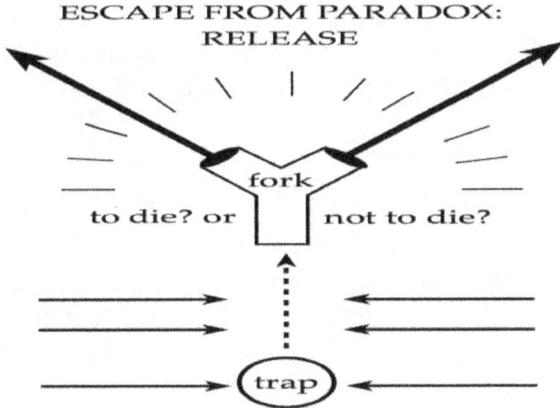

Recall the *ESCAPE FROM PARADOX* diagram presented and explained in *BOOK ONE*, and pictured again on the previous page.

This idea, that we can be sensitive to forks in our roads, even before these are obvious to us, is key here. Let's pause a moment to think about what this means.

1) Every day, we make little and big decisions. We have to, as this is part of living. We decide what to eat, whether to take a walk, what time to go to bed, and so on. We also decide what may be less obvious matters such as how to feel about something, what we say next, what little movement or intention we express even subconsciously, and so on.

2) We can think in terms of living as moving, moment to moment, through decisions. The more we are aware of our patterned processes and of what I have described as the ***energy textures and arrangements*** – these and other key characteristics of the *PATTERN TERRAIN* -- we are moving through as we live, the more we can have a say in how we *NAVIGATE OUR LIVES*.

3) Note again: This does not mean we can change everything that happens around and to us, however this does mean we can have increasing say in how we respond, how we experience all this. WE ARE THUS EVER MORE CONSCIOUSLY NAVIGATING OUR EXPERIENCE OF LIVING, OR BEING.

Now, let's go back to this fork in the road concept....

Usually, prior to coming to a fork in our road, or a window of opportunity, is the arrival at a need for shedding, shedding part or all of a pattern.

Being at this point involves several decisions we may or may not be prepared to, or aware enough to, make. First, we must decide to be this aware. Second, we must decide to realize there are choices, decisions we can make. These decisions include doing nothing different or new, staying on the same path, in the same pattern. Even doing nothing, staying in the same pattern, is a decision.

Third, we must decide to make whatever decision we make as consciously as we can, to pull ourselves out of automatic as much as we can. Fourth, we must see what the options are. Fifth, we must select, decide upon, our options.

All this is part of finding ourselves at the windows of opportunity and yes, at the forks in our roads.

As in our being programmed not to readily be detecting forks and windows, we tend to miss seeing that we need to shed our skins, let go what we can of our problem patterns, until we are either...

- deep into needing to shed, or perhaps ...
- deep into an actual shedding process, or are ...
- already completed with the process, or are ...
- well into a much later shedding.

- Or, we entirely miss our sheddings, not realizing that these have taken place, which results in our not using sheddings (pattern deaths) well, and or not bringing these to healthier completion.

- We have the opportunity *consciously harvest* our energy from patterns we choose to change and or shed.

- So often, we start to change and then are pulled right back into the old pattern we were attempting to leave, to change out of. We fall back into, we slip, we crash, we fall, perhaps we relapse.

But shedding part or all of a pattern, pattern system (or pattern set or cluster) is as much a part of life and death as is any other function. You shed skin cells and hair every day. If you are an adult, you have, most likely, already shed some habits, relationships, addictions, behaviors.

NAVIGATION KEY
IDENTIFY THE FORK IN THE ROAD
PRODUCING THE PARADOX TRAP

Sometimes it is the obvious or hidden fork in the road itself that reveals an exit option. The pressure of the *PARADOXical trap*, the forces and factors working against each other, blocking each other from moving into a new form of themselves, of their patterns, form the *PARADOX trap*.

We feel this trap, we feel the stuck, locked, difficult to move feeling. We do not feel comfortable in such a place.

→ → → stuck, trapped ← ← ←

What is the way out of this situation? Sometimes this involves being highly alert to the sensations themselves.

WE WANT TO BE CLEAR WITH OURSELVES HERE:

SOME PROBLEM PATTERNS SEEK TO TRAP OUR ENERGY INTO THEMSELVES, AND CAN APPLY THESE HOLDING PATTERNS TO HOLD US TRAPPED.

OTHER PATTERNS FALL INTO THE PARADOXical STATE ALMOST RANDOMLY WHEN PATTERN AGENDAS FALL INTO OPPOSITION OF, OR CONFLICT WITH, EACH OTHER.

PARADOXical STATES, WHEN RECOGNIZED AS ENERGY-LADEN PARADOX PATTERNS, CAN BE CONSCIOUSLY NAVIGATED TO MOVE, TO ELEVATE, TO A HIGHER LEVEL OF AWARENESS AND MORE COMMAND OF THE ENERGY TRAPPED IN THE PARADOX PATTERN.

Quite often, we are sensing these *PARADOX* patterns, these *energy traps,* prior to knowing we are feeling the sensations of our energy being trapped. We can turn up our radar, we can increase our sensitivity and be on the lookout for sensations that may not yet have words or even definitions labelling them.

Some ways out of energy traps are physical. However, many are emotional, mental, even for some, spiritual.

The sense or sensation of a trap is an energetic sense, sensation. As per the *ESCAPE FROM PARADOX* diagram pictured earlier, we are sometimes caught in the pressure of the *PARADOX trap*. As this pressure builds, there can appear to be two of more choices, a to-do or not-to-do sensation, an energetic tug of war. The choice appears, quite frequently as a sensing of a fork in the road, even before the specifics of the choices or options available are clear.

Form a picture of this in your mind, a picture of being on a road where you come to a fork. This fork can present two or more pathways, directions you can choose from. Allow yourself to see these options. Enter into at least one of the pathways led to by the fork in the road. If you do not see these, sense these, even imagine, visualize, these to get to know these.

One or more of the entries into these forks in the road are exit doors, exits from the PARADOX trap that, in its pressure, has revealed this fork in your road. One of the entries likely leads right back into the same road you have been traveled, the same pattern you have been within.

NAVIGATION KEY
SENSITIZE TO
PATTERN DESTRUCTERING OPTIONS

It is best to recognize and de-structure detrimental patterns before they become physical. It is best to ever more consciously, alertly, *NAVIGATE LIFE'S STUFF*, life's patterns, and *your programming to be patterned.*

This means that we must be looking for, sensing aspects of, our patterns well before they make themselves visible, explicit, to the physical eye. This means that feeling situations on a sensory, even non- or pre- verbal, even precognitive (subconscious) level, of the *personal radar* is essential. Yes, we have the basic five senses of seeing, hearing, smelling, tasting, touching. We can also generate within ourselves other senses, other levels of awareness.

Much more is accomplished when the work is done above (or outside) the level of the physical body and plane. Whatever you, Reader, choose to imagine that this is, your awareness of, conscious travel through, even surgery on, your energy patterns is possible and essential.

(For many people, this is simply using imagination and visualization, and applying metaphor. And this is already calling the attention of the mind and brain. Physical, biological, and electrical brain activity actually engages in imagination, visualization, and metaphor developing thought patterns. In this way, we are already bringing work done beyond the physical body into the physical body.[18])

****

***Sensitizing** ourselves to the nature and characteristics of our experience of living, seeing what this journey is (on a psychological and or psycho-spiritual basis, and **on the level of the personal consciousness**), is essential in consciously NAVIGATING LIFE'S STUFF, in moving through the PATTERN TERRAIN.*

---

[18] I explain this process in greater depth, and even diagram this process, in other books in this *KEYS TO CONSCIOUSNESS AND SURVIVAL SERIES*, such as *UNVEILING THE HIDDEN INSTINCT* and *HOW TO DIE AND SURVIVE*.

Ultimately it is <u>your</u> experience of <u>your</u> life that is <u>your</u> LIFE'S STUFF.

Let me say this again and again: We cannot control everything that happens in the world, not even everything that happens to <u>us</u>. However, we can have a say in how we see and experience and move through, NAVIGATE, what happens within and around us.

PART TEN

KEYS IN NAVIGATING RELEASE, ELEVATION, TRANSCENDENCE

**Chapter 35
Navigating Release:
Harvesting Your SELF in
Your Changes and Transitions**

This chapter delves ever more deeply into the matter of our **programmed-in resistance** *to change, and how much of our energy is locked into this resistance.*

This is the pattern itself taking energy to sustain itself, to protect itself from being shed. *Whether this is a healthy pattern or an unhealthy (problem) pattern,* **the pattern is designed to do what it takes to preserve itself.**

This is about how our programming to develop patterns includes our programming to sustain, to protect, the patterns themselves, to resist shedding these patterns, even to carry the deeply embedded and stubborn patterning to be **resistant to change**. *The issue becomes one of how we NAVIGATE our way through, even out of,* **our resistance to change** *when well being, even survival, may depend upon this change. Understanding this resistance, and how deeply embedded into us is this resistance, is key here.*

<u>RELEASE KEY</u>
*DETECT PATTERN OF
RESISTANCE, OF PARADOX*

This resistance to change holds, traps, energy right into a *pattern of resistance*, a stuck place, a *PARADOX* pattern. (See again BOOK ONE of NAVIGATING LIFE'S STUFF where the *PARADOX pattern*, among four basic core patterns, is defined.) It is in this state of *PARADOX*, in this *PARADOX* pattern, that forces can stand off against each other, push against each other.

This PARADOX pattern emerges when forces and factors conflict or press against each other, have <u>competing pattern purposes</u> (e.g., what sustains one pattern diminishes or threatens the sustaining of the other pattern and vice versa – and or, what sustains one pattern diminishes or threatens the pattern system of the host of the pattern).

For example, an unhealthy pattern may be programmed to fight to sustain itself, to survive, while this pattern threatens surrounding healthy patterns, even the life of the host of this pattern. Again, the simple *PARADOX pattern* looks and feels something like this:

The *PARADOXical **pattern of resistance to change*** encompasses itself, the *PARADOX pattern itself*, as well as the other and or sub-patterns it is protecting (resisting the change away from or the death of), and also the other patterns it is subsuming, trapping within itself.

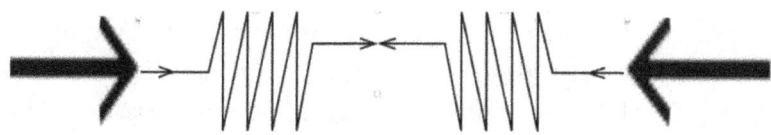

PARADOXical Pattern Trap

This pattern trap (→ ←) holds the patterns within (⋙ ⋘) it, locked in the PARADOXical trap of resistance to change.

If we listen we can hear, if we sensitize, we can feel, the resistance present in the *PARADOX* trap. Be aware of what you are telling yourself, of what you are reading regarding your environment. Yes, be aware of your surroundings, but also of your inner environment where your patterns are at work.

It is within your inner environment that the PATTERN TERRAIN can mesh with you, dominate you, even obscure your access to your SELF. Watch for these energy patterns and pattern trends deep within your mind, below your level of conscious awareness.

You can pull this knowing more and more into your conscious level by understanding that this is taking place – and designed to be taking place – outside your awareness.

Choosing to ever more sensitize yourself to what is taking place deep within you is a positive and empowering choice. You can begin to see where there are productive situations where patterns are healthy for their hosts, for you. You can also begin to see, earlier and earlier, EVEN LONG BEFORE THEIR PROBLEM EFFECTS SURFACE, where patterns are not healthy for their hosts, for you. What I am talking about here is the reality that *this awareness of the, your, PATTERN TERRAIN,* can be enhanced, greatly empowered. The PATTERN TERRAIN you move through can be NAVIGATED with ever greater attention, alertness, and care.

Imagine you have sensors, sub-sub microscopic level readers, reading any pressures, tensions, constraints upon your SELF, even upon your awareness. Give these pressures, tensions, constraints, characteristics, **ways you can notice** *these when they are present, even when these are difficult to detect or even waiting in the wings so to speak. Form your own markers for these, images or mental icons or sensations of some sort, that you can use to identify these in your mind and in your awareness, as these appear and re-appear over time. These are your markers for you to use while NAGIVATING the patterning and PATTERN TERRAIN that occupies, inhabits, you.*

Now imagine, or visualize, or find in your way, any actual patterns of resistance to change.

Look to see whether you have already, previously, perhaps even concurrently, placed any identifying markers right within the patterns' resistance to you, to your SELF.

Also look for any <u>markers within</u> the resistance to change patterns that these patterns are forming. These patterns have identifying markers, or we can give these patterns such markers in our minds.

This is a subtle concept, one requiring our imagination and visualization tools to begin its process:

Can you see, or imagine you see, **these markers indicating the presence of these patterns of resistance to change***, even resistance to* <u>*your*</u> *changing or* <u>*leaving*</u> *a particular problem pattern? You can come face to face with the pattern of resistance fighting you.*

Now imagine, visualize, elements of the pattern's texture, such as the pattern's energy grid, rays, vectors, and tendrils, working their way through your mind, or through other of your patterns. Look also for pattern density and pattern knots.

Allow yourself to feel that the moment you identify these markers, the moment you detect and then give yourself a way of spotting them again, you have already taken some energy from the PARADOX trap in that your own awareness requires energy to be aware.

<u>**RELEASE KEY**</u>
SENSE PROGRAMMING
TO RESIST CHANGE,
TO STAY HELD IN, STUCK IN, PATTERNS

At times we are quite aware we are resisting change. Other times, we are resisting change yet doing so subconsciously, on some level we are not fully aware of. Our programming to develop patterns includes programming to hold patterns in place. In this sense, we are programmed not to change or break a pattern unless pressured to, perhaps even forced to, by some factor or overriding program.

Frequently, a healthy pattern replaces a previously healthy but outdated or drained pattern, the newer healthy pattern making way for itself.

How very frequently problem patterns and addictions to problem patterns are in place, and are resisting change away from these problem patterns, and their problem pattern addiction or sustain functions.

Readers who may be dealing with problem emotional, and also mental (such as cognitive), also behavioral, and or physical patterns can feel how deeply instilled problem patterns can be. This makes change difficult, and makes change feel difficult, even at times unpleasant. *(Again: The PARADOX, the conflicting pressures, are the pattern **pressure to sustain** itself versus **pressure to override and shed** the problem pattern:* → ←.*)*

Even when a positive change (such as moving out of a problem pattern into a healthy pattern) may be underway, a *STRUGGLE pattern*, one resisting or even blocking this change, may in effect be waged by the problem pattern resisting its being amended or entirely shed.

Again, we carry deep within ourselves programming to stay stuck in patterns, whether these are healthy patterns or problem, troubled, and or dangerous patterns. This staying stuck is ADDICTION itself.

In this sense, this addiction function is central in the pattern sustain function. **We are all addicts to some degree, all programmed by our patterns to grow addicted to our patterns.**

NAVIGATING LIFE'S STUFF can be, and ideally must be, done with increasing *awareness of the states of our patterns and the pressures our patterns carry to hold us stuck within our patterns*. Again here, I say that **we are all programmed to become addicted to our patterns: we all carry this programming in our systems.**

Given that this programming exists (one assumes) to maintain healthy life sustaining patterns, I see this programming that also protects <u>problem</u> patterns as a ***glitch in the system, in our system***.[19]

What this means is that when we are resisting change, *our patterns are resisting* our changing out of these particular patterns. Working our way out of the underlying core patterns of the *STRUGGLE* itself or of the *PARADOXical trap* we can *fall into* – **are designed to fall into** – *are programmed to fall into under control of our patterning itself* -- involves seeing what is happening here.

We are programmed to get stuck and to stay stuck, in patterns, even in and especially in problem patterns. We are likely even programmed, perhaps via a ***glitch in our system***, to form stubborn problem patterns as these control us so effectively.

---

[19] I have discussed this glitch in our systems in greater depth in other books in this *KEYS TO CONSCIOUSNESS AND SURVIVAL SERIES,* such as *UNVEILING THE HIDDEN INSTINCT* and *OVERIDING THE EXTINCTION SCENARIO.* See recommended reading at the end of this book. See also the book, *SEEING THE HIDDEN FACE OF ADDICTION.*

RELEASE KEY
SENSE RESISTANCE TO CHANGE

Again and again, we can grow ever more aware that: We are programmed to develop patterns and then to preserve the patterns we develop, to resist changing out of our existing patterns. These patterns are repeat processes we are programmed to become habituated to, addicted to. Therefore, NAVIGATING our way out of these problem patterns, NAVIGATING our way into change, involves our seeing what is happening to us.

Our resistance to change, even our relapsing into existing patterns, habits, addictions we may want to leave or break, is *a pattern sustaining process programmed deeply into us*. We are creatures of habit, of addiction, by nature.

We therefore, whether or not we want to, find change out of our problem patterns to be inconvenient, and or agitating, destabilizing, overwhelming, or even threatening, often even feeling a little (or a lot) like some sort of dying process. Rather than feel change is an opportunity to shift oneself into a new aspect of oneself, a new dimension of one's reality, a new reality—on a deep patterning level, particular change may feel like a bad thing, and yes, even a little like dying.

Old patterns die hard. The death of a pattern is not easily achieved, as change is resisted by the pattern itself. Yet, the more we see ourselves as programmed to resist changing out of problem patterns, the more we can see what is happening to us when we resist: we are programmed to resist.

Chapter 36
Release Awareness

Being consciously aware of our programming, of our highly programmed-in patternings, can help us find our way through the maze of our realities, of our minds, of our situations.

To bring our greater awareness of our programming to NAVIGATING our LIFE's STUFF, is to enlighten ourselves. This will allow us to see where we need not resist moving out of old patterns, where we need not resist the flow of the life force throughout ourselves, where we can open to a recognition of this flow and to a movement with this flow.

RELEASE AWARENESS KEY
BEING HIGHLY AWARE

Whatever your sense of a higher power or a divine force within yourself, you can tap into this. No one belief system is required to do this. The greater your understanding of this dynamic force for growth and change you carry within you, the more your actions, your response to patterns, can harmonize with this—can harmonize with who you truly are which is not your patterns, not your programming.

This greater and *more conscious understanding* of what is going on when you are stuck in patterns, patterns you want to or need to change or leave, helps you to fortify your awareness and is essential. This greater understanding will also help you ward off, even prevent, the taking or "kidnapping" of your energy by these undesirable encroaching patterns.

Just as there are predators in the jungle, there are forces (pattern programmings) in all dimensions of our minds and realities which seek to use our energy arrangements and transitions and releases for their own purposes.

RELEASE AWARENESS KEY
PREPARING FOR THE HARVEST

The process of NAVIGATING LIFE'S STUFF is about what it means to take your energy back: to find your own energy for yourself, to release your energy to your SELF, even that energy that has been trapped in problem patterns.

This is about your being able to detect and then *harvest your energy for your SELF*. This is your energy that has been locked into patterns that require your energy to sustain these patterns, to hold these patterns in place.

Remember, your energy is yours, not your patterns' energy. You can choose to have increasing awareness and say regarding what your energy is, does, and where it goes, what patterns it feeds. This is consciously NAVIGATING your LIFE'S STUFF.

This means that you, as a responsible being, must learn to be highly sensitive to, ever more aware of, the flow of your energy in and out of patterns, in and out of situations, in and out of passages (such pattern crises, pattern transitions, pattern endings, pattern deaths). You must be as aware as possible, as conscious of what is going on as you can be.

You can see the patterns and pattern clusters that you have been living by, even trapped within. **WHICH OF THESE YOU CHOOSE TO LIVE BY IS UP TO YOU.**

<u>*RELEASE AWARENESS KEY*</u>
WATCH FOR
PATTERN EXIT OPTIONS, WINDOWS

You must be ever alert for moments when you can see what is going on, and see how to exit a pattern, how to SHED a pattern segment or pattern or cluster of patterns that have been *occupying you.*

You can take yourself back by learning to be ever more sensitive to the moments, places, times when you can LEAP[20] out of a pattern that has been holding you trapped, stuck, captive.

You can sensitize to opportunities to move out of, break free of, release yourself from, <u>**transcend**,</u> *problem patterns. You can learn to sense forks in your road, and* **windows opening to your changes, or possible changes, windows in your mind, in your own personal reality.**

Here, as change can itself feel like a good thing, or can feel neutral, or not so good, or at times like a crisis, you can benefit by learning to be as aware as you can as you NAGIVATE your changes, transitions, endings, pattern deaths. Learn to stay as conscious as you can through all

---

[20] I have defined this *LEAP* in several books in this *KEYS TO CONSCIOUSNESS AND SURVIVAL SERIES* such as *HOW TO DIE AND SURVIVE* and *UNVEILING THE HIDDEN INSTINCT*. See recommended reading listed at the end of this book.

your endings and pattern deaths—physical and non-physical, emotional and otherwise.

Grow *ever more aware of* the *patterns occupying you*, harnessing your energy, as you move to amend, change, shift, or leave these patterns.

When changing, shifting to a modified or new pattern or pattern system, allow yourself to feel the energy at play, the energy you can take back from a pattern that has held it trapped in that pattern itself.

And, as you do move your energy out of an old pattern or cluster of patterns, be very aware of your energy, in order to be certain you do not surrender, sign over, or land your energy in a new place where you (perhaps again) lose say, lose Free Will, over its use.

Do not automatically shift from one pattern into another pattern without knowing you have a say, a conscious say, in your patterning.

It is your responsibility then to prepare for the appropriate and conscious harvest of your own energy which takes place during and following each and every one of your pattern changes, shifts, transitions, and endings.

<u>RELEASE AWARENESS KEY</u>
DETECT OPPORTUNITIES TO HARVEST YOUR SELF

To best prepare for your harvest, *your harvest of yourself* AS YOU TAKE YOUR SELF BACK, **take control of your life.** Although you can not control all the events around you, you can direct, *NAVIGATE*, ever more of your process, your ride through these patterns and their processes.

- Become sensitive to the feel of the *PATTERN TERRAIN* such as pattern phases, sheddings, forks, windows, and exits as described in previous chapters.

- During any complex or difficult pattern shift or transition, indeed during any pattern shift or transition whether or not difficult, stay focused.

  Define for yourself what this focus will mean for you.

  For example, you may choose to stay focused on a high point within what you feel is your physical body, or a metaphor for a physical body. You may want to select either the area in the center of the forehead or at the top of the head to stay connected to.

- *Understand that the focus you hold on to is your SELF, not* your patterning. You are thus seeking to hold on to your *SELF* as you *NAVIGATE* your life. This focus, your focus, is your connection to YOU.[21]

- Hold on to this connection, keep returning to the idea of it, as if there were a cord attached to it, no matter what happens.

---

[21] For exercises helping to develop this personal focus, see *Volume 3* in this *KEYS TO CONSCIOUSNESS AND SURVIVAL SERIES*, titled *UNVEILING THE HIDDEN INSTINCT*.

- Think of your connection to your focus, to your *SELF*, as being sometimes directly on point or on spot. Other times, you may connect to your *SELF* from a conceptual distance, perhaps by what you visualize as being energetic or conceptual rays or arms or tendrils.

- Think of your connections to your *SELF* as those you can imagine that you weave through your patterns. See your connections to your *SELF* perhaps as your own personal rays or tendrils or cords from *YOU* to your *SELF*.

  Know which these are, which of what you sense is out there in the *PATTERN TERRAIN* are part of you, your *SELF*. You want to continuously be aware of the distinction between yourself and the patterns inhabiting you, as problem patterns will seek to deceive you, to hold you away from *YOU*, to allow you to feel you are connected to your *SELF* when you are connected to the problem pattern posing as you.

- You will always have the option of not staying connected to your focus, to your *SELF*. This is your right to choose this option. You can let go of your *SELF* and give way to the flow or, direction of, any particular patterning that is occupying you. Just try to know you are doing so, so that the conscious choice is yours. Do not let problem patterns decide this for you.

- To say this again here: If you want to let go of this connection from you to your *SELF*, to let go of this tendril or cord, you can. But do so quite consciously, as if you are knowingly releasing the reigns while riding a wild horse.

  And do check out the *PATTERN TERRAIN* beforehand. Are there any traps or trick windows leading to dead ends or undesirable nests for your energy? Is this where you want to be? If not, these trick nests, these dead ends, must be avoided.

- **KEEP YOUR OWN COUNSEL. Notice when you may be being pulled in a direction against your will.**

- Try to see and sense what is calling you and coming at you. (Another book in this *KEYS TO CONSCIOUSNESS AND SURVIVAL Series* will detail the various releases of the cord that you might undertake at this juncture.[22] For now, letting go, yet being conscious as you do, is enough of a description.)

- Again, giving way to positive and negative patterns inhabiting you, is your choice. Just know this as you *NAVIGATE*. Let your *SELF* decide.

---

[22] See the *HOW TO DIE AND SURVIVE* books in this *KEYS TO CONSCIOUSNESS AND SURVIVAL Series*.

RELEASE AWARENESS KEY
KEEP YOUR OWN COUNSEL

Examine information for truth. We must do this. Truth has been distorted by language and culture.

The precious consciousness of Humanity is buried within an elaborate hierarchy of distortion which veils too much truth. *Human words and beliefs are part of this elaborate distortion.* We, our minds, are programmed to fall into line, to fit the overall patterning our species has been given.

Tell yourself what a spiritual truth is for you. This may or may not be related to religion, this is up to you. *Your spirit is your spirit, however you choose to define this.*

A spiritual truth, to be honestly relayed in its wholeness, can not be distorted. A spiritual truth, without ever being intellectualized by the brain, can congeal into an experience, an awareness, an image or a symbol.

That experience, awareness or image can again unfold in the eye of its beholder, depending upon the sophistication of the beholder, in terms of his or her readiness, into varying degrees of truth.

Let this unfolding begin within you. When you are ready to understand your truth, to be sure that what your patterns allow you to know of your truth is actually *YOUR TRUTH*, you will recognize your truth as it comes to you.

RELEASE AWARENESS KEY
SEE THE POWER IN
KNOWING WHO YOU ARE

Continue to strive to know who you truly are. Know that every individual soul is a micro-consciousness, one which affects the overarching. macro-consciousness. Every soul vibrates at its own frequency of consciousness. This frequency can be raised—evolved by that soul. Spiritual evolution is a constant developing of form, spiritual form.

You may want to view this process of *NAVIGATION* this way:

The sole purpose of any consciousness or spirit coming into the third dimension of reality is to work toward manifesting what is in some belief systems called the "indwelling spirit."

Find your own views of what it means to you to be alive, to exist. Decide for your *SELF* who you are. Do not let the patterns inhabiting you, or the programming driving those patterns, tell you who you are.

Chapter 37
Releasing Energy, SELVES,
From Pattern-Locks and Pattern-Traps:
Becoming the Phoenix and Rising

Let's add another layer of understanding to the DYNAMICS OF PERSONAL CHANGE offered in these NAVIGATING LIFE'S STUFF books.

Note that the previous book, BOOK ONE of NAVIGATING LIFE'S STUFF, defined four basic core patterns: STRUGGLE, PARADOX, INSIGHT, and ELEVATION. These patterns underly and accompany many if not all of our emotional and behavioral patterns.

Here, in this chapter, the ELEVATION pattern is considered as a profound shift in awareness, a TRANSCENDENCE.

<u>*NAVIGATION RELEASE ELEVATION*</u>
ELEVATION TO TRANSCENDENCE OF PATTERNS

The *ELEVATION* pattern is present when an actual and lasting shift or change out of pattern or pattern system does take place. This is the transcendence of patterns, the transcendence of the *STRUGGLE* and *PARADOX patterns* at the core of so much of our emotions and behaviors.

This is also the sustaining of the brief glimpse of a way the way out of a pattern, the sustaining of the *INSIGHT pattern*, which itself does not reach actual *ELEVATION*.

Note these diagrams of *INSIGHT pattern* and *ELEVATION pattern* here. (See *BOOK ONE* for definitions of these core patterns: *STRUGGLE, PARADOX, INSIGHT, ELEVATION*.)

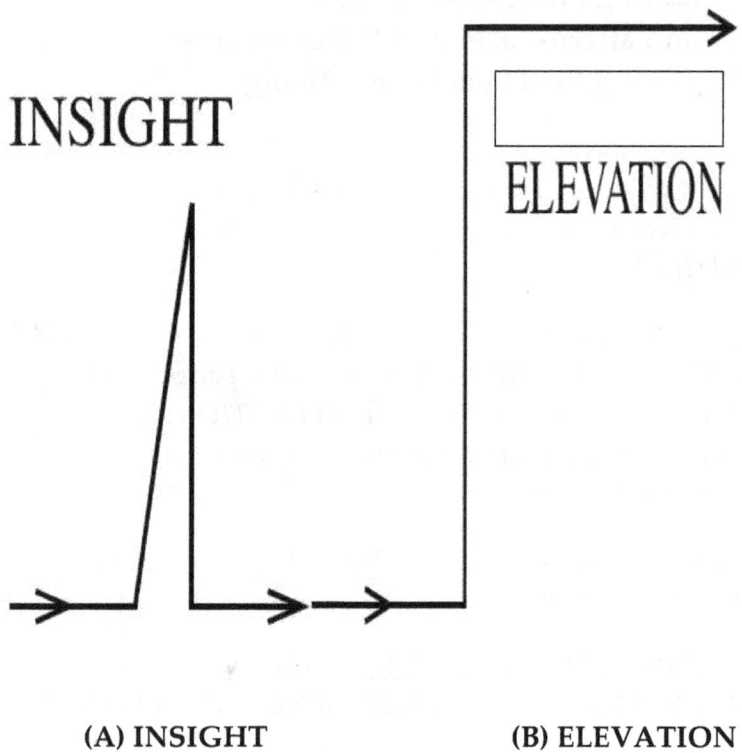

(A) INSIGHT   (B) ELEVATION

The two core patterns diagrammed above represent: (A) the brief increase in awareness, the *INSIGHT pattern*, that is not sustained; and (B) the sustaining of that increase in awareness, the *ELEVATION pattern*.

Ideally, understanding how to shift out of problem patterns, how to *ELEVATE* away from problem patterns, increases as one experiences this and is aware of what this is.

When we are consciously *NAVIGATING* our way through our patterns, and can change away from problem patterns with sustained change, *ELEVATED* change, this is indeed a *TRANSCENDENCE of patterning*. (See again *BOOK ONE* for more on the *ELEVATION* pattern.)

NAVIGATION RELEASE ELEVATION
KNOW THE PHOENIX IMAGERY
AS ELEVATION, TRANSCENDENCE

Consider the popular mythology of the Phoenix, the bird who rises from the ashes, from the spoils, from the remains of an apocalypse, the bird whose egg is hatched in the heat of that cataclysmic global fire and rises in full splendor. In essence, the Phoenix rising is you.

This mythology, so popular among indigenous and ancient cultures, is an important transference of an understanding that you can move through personal pattern change and transition. It is your choice, *how* you rise and what form you will take when you rise or *ELEVATE*.

The vision of the Phoenix rising from the ashes permeates many teachings around the world. The Phoenix is often described as having a rainbow or multiple-colored coat, with shiny blue-purple (or indigo) feathers on its wings, long red and bluish tail feathers, gold neck feathers, light-colored feathers on its head, and a tuft of various colors at the back of its head, giving it the appearance of being two-headed.

Most ancient mystics viewed the Phoenix as symbolic of the immortality of the soul. Initiates into mystery schools who were considered to have been reborn were raised to the level of what was often called "phoenix."

Egyptian mythology describes what it calls the "Ka" as the Egyptian "bennu" or phoenix bird: Ka often appears to the deceased in the form of a blue phoenix, offering the recently physically dead person (the "Ba," or lower self), the opportunity to rejoin her or his "Ka," or higher self, who is also the eternal mother. In such belief systems, the shock and release of death can trigger this "divine union" and the uniting of the so-called "lower self" with the so-called "higher spirit." (I leave it to Readers to define all this in their own terms, according to their own belief systems.)

To absorb the message that the story of the Phoenix holds for you, you must take your *SELF* through a process of increasing sensitization.

NAVIGATION RELEASE ELEVATION
VISUALIZE: BURNING DOWN

Now, with your eyes closed, visualize yourself in a house which is on fire. First, you see the smoke coming at you from all directions. Then, you see the flames surrounding you. The flames are large and dancing before your eyes. The flames are blue and red and orange and yellow. They are gold. Gold. Gold.

The intensity of the fire increases. Yet it is not heat, not physically hot per se. Still, you feel the energy of the burn. You even sense you almost sizzle. You may feel as if you are being boiled without water, without being immersed in water. You are rising to a higher intensity, temperature of SELF, and this does not burn you, rather, with conscious NAVIGATION, this ELEVATES your energy.

Do not look away from these feelings. Notice to what degree you go into these feelings. Notice to what degree you keep yourself distanced from the sensations that would be attached to this experience if it were happening in reality.

Notice how much or how little you feel about this image; notice how much resistance you have to the feelings. Ask yourself: Would this response, the degree of involvement in this process, be different were you surrounded right now by real flames, a real fire?

Allow your energy to survive the conceptual heat. What is igniting is old forms and formats, old patterns. These patterns are not you, as YOU, yourSELF, are not dissolving.

Imagine your SELF, your awareness, transforming, transcending, from physical to nonphysical versions of your SELF, and back and forth through this process again and again.

Notice that through all this, you are still aware of yourself. Notice that, as your problem patterns dissolve, there is a point when some part of problem patterning that might have endured now disappears.

In your imagination, stay dissolved a moment. You are still looking at this scene, but from outside of it. Who are you now? Examine yourSELF, what are your characteristics?

After noting your characteristics, see yourSELF, or what remains of your physicality, crumbling to smoldering ashes. Hold this image for the following exercise....

NAVIGATION RELEASE ELEVATION
VISUALIZE: PHOENIX RISING

Stay crumbled, disintegrated in smoldering ash. Feel your SELF, your consciousness, observing this scene. Think of your consciousness as floating above this scene, looking down on it.

Now take your consciousness, your SELF, down into the ash. Collect your consciousness under the ashes. Collect your consciousness into an egg-like capsule. Fold up tightly within this capsule, in a fetal position, for several minutes. While you are folded up in there, begin thinking about cracking out of the egg. Feel as if you are a marvelous bird about to be born. As you expand with this egg-like capsule, you feel it cracking open just a bit. As the capsule cracks open, you realize that this is no longer an egg, if it ever was one.

Continue becoming a marvelous bird, a beautiful Phoenix, however you imagine a Phoenix to look. Suddenly, your vehicle bursts open. You unfold your wings as you stand. You spread your wings and rise.

****

Hold on to the vision of yourself as the Phoenix rising from the dust or ashes, or remnants of problem patterns. This can be the imagery of survival, the vision of resurrection which can transport you into your own personal *ELEVATION pattern*, into TRANSCENDENCE OF PROBLEM PATTERNS.

Recognize yourself as *YOUR OWN PERSONAL VEHICLE, YOUR OWN PERSONAL PHOENIX*. Always feel that this triumphant rising from the ashes can be yours. Embrace the Phoenix — this is you.

When you fully embrace the death of a problem pattern, as being your *ELEVATION* into your own *TRANSCENDENCE*, you will know. You will set the captive free. You will *ELEVATE YOUR FOCUS, YOUR SELF, YOUR FORCE OF WILL*, and fly through the portal of change into new patterns, new formats of your *SELF*.

You will rise from the ashes of challenge, transition, *STRUGGLE* and *PARADOX*, in splendor: the Phoenix *transcending*, sustaining the *INSIGHT*, the Phoenix *ELEVATING*.

Chapter 38
Epilog:
Becoming a Spirit-Driven Revolutionary, Driven by Your Own Spirit of Your SELF

We are programmed, designed, to be caught in, trapped in, even addicted to, patterns that control us. For the most part, these are healthy patterns, and this is good, even essential programming. However, as this book has discussed, when these are problem patterns holding us caught in, trapped in, addicted to, these patterns, we have a problem.

PROGRAMMED PEOPLE

Programmed people are not free; they are biological robots proceeding to function as programmed. Whatever bit of the *SELF* nestles within the heart of a problem pattern addicted being is to some degree trapped, caged, maybe suffocating.

Too many people find themselves to be harmed, even suffocated by, the problem patternings that inhabit them. These patterns may eventually permanently extinguish some of these people.

Any master plan of evolution, or of any intelligent design, that would have planned for this development, if you believe there is one, must be overthrown—or at least better understood. Too many souls are being enslaved, turned into robots, lost. The massive stagnating and extinguishing of the Free Will of the Human spirit threatens Humanity.

You become a sort of revolutionary when you master your awareness and *NAVIGATION* of the patternings inhabiting you. This is because the limits to your reality, your prison walls, will be broken through by you, your *SELF*.

CAPTAIN YOUR JOURNEY

Were each and every one of us able to ride personal, social, and global challenge and change; even personal, social, and global disaster; personal, social, and global apocalypse; personal, social, and global death, *into empowered awareness and power*, we could be an ever more powerful people. We would be more powerful as individuals and as a *collective life force*.

DYNAMIC NAVIGATION

I am inviting you to become exactly this: conscious captain of your own journey, master of the patterns inhabiting you, master of the challenges, changes, transitions, minor and major problem pattern deaths, you see and experience. This can, if you wish, enable you to master your life. After all, we are always living and dying. And so is our world.

RETHINK

Rethink the concept of our patterning, our pattern transitions, pattern endings, even pattern deaths. Look at how controlled we are by our programming to be patterned. Do this for yourself and for all Humanity. Your—our—survival, *our freedom from control of us by our programming* to be patterned, depends upon the spreading of this awareness.

You will grow to understand this on a deep level as you read through these *NAVIGATING LIFE'S STUFF: DYNAMICS OF PERSONAL CHANGE* books, and the other books in this *KEYS TO CONSCIOUSNESS AND SURVIVAL SERIES*. These ideas about pattern transition and pattern death processes will flow gently into your consciousness, and will allow you to take them as lightly or profoundly as you wish — as you feel ready to.

This journey is yours. So make it your own. Master the ride of your life. Meet challenge: recognize even the deepest programming we carry, even the most deeply implanted patterns of living, of thinking, of experiencing, even patterns of confusion, crisis, change, transition, and death, all kinds of death. Consciously *NAVIGATE* patterns and come to know so much more about your *SELF*.

The time has indeed come for the removal of our ignorance, for the removal of the blinders we have been led to believe we must carry, that *we are programmed to carry.*

We *can* know more, as much more as we are ready to know, about what is happening to us, within and around us — about who we truly are.

KEYS TO CONSCIOUSLY MOVING THROUGH OUR PROCESSES AND THEIR PATTERNS

APPENDICES

KEYS TO CONSCIOUSLY MOVING THROUGH OUR PROCESSES AND THEIR PATTERNS

Appendix A
KEYS TO
CONSCIOUSNESS
AND SURVIVAL SERIES

Series Foreword

Just as the fish itself did not discover water, we ourselves have perhaps inadvertently demonstrated the obvious, which is that we cannot entirely, absolutely, know what all it is "we" are immersed in, nor even what all it is that "we" are.

Ultimately, the question of the hour, the question of our times, the question of our reality, is regarding this "thing" we call our "consciousness." How do we identify with our consciousness, is it of us, is it us, is it more than we are, or is it simply a side effect of life? While this term, **consciousness***, appears in a multitude of contexts, is even part of the popular jargon, what consciousness is and means remains unsettled, unproven, disputed. The full nature of consciousness itself is, even after centuries of Human discussion, still eluding us.*

I suggest that the true question here is whether the amorphous consciousness is itself derivative of biology, or is itself independent of biology (and perhaps even independent of what any intelligence can entirely discover of itself from within itself and its tools). I add, however, that even this question will reveal itself to be irrelevant. This stunning shift *in understanding will happen once we recognize that our seemingly elusive consciousness can at any point be redefined, or step forward and **redefine itself to itself and thus to us**—or even shift into (or back into) independence of biology, stepping out of evolutionary, synaptic, and conceptual controls. Once consciousness steps forward, moves into its existence <u>independent</u> of Human science, religion, philosophy, **even of the Human brain itself**— consciousness may (perhaps once again) elect to leave our physical bodies, much like a grown child leaving home.*

As they depart, we can speculate that our consciousness-es are in a sense like our children, in that they apparently stem from us—a speculation no machine intelligence (as yet incapable of actual procreation and actual biological parental ties) will ever do unless consciously programmed to be able to do. Our children, once they consciously leave home, their consciousness-es in tow, can grow up to consciously be who they already are.

*Get ready, even the Human Consciousness is going to break free of the **conceptual** confines of its biological host bodies here on Earth. It's been a nice visit but the time may come to go, or at least **expand our awareness**.*

Dr. Angela Brownemiller

Appendix B
Concepts of Differing Levels of Awareness and Body

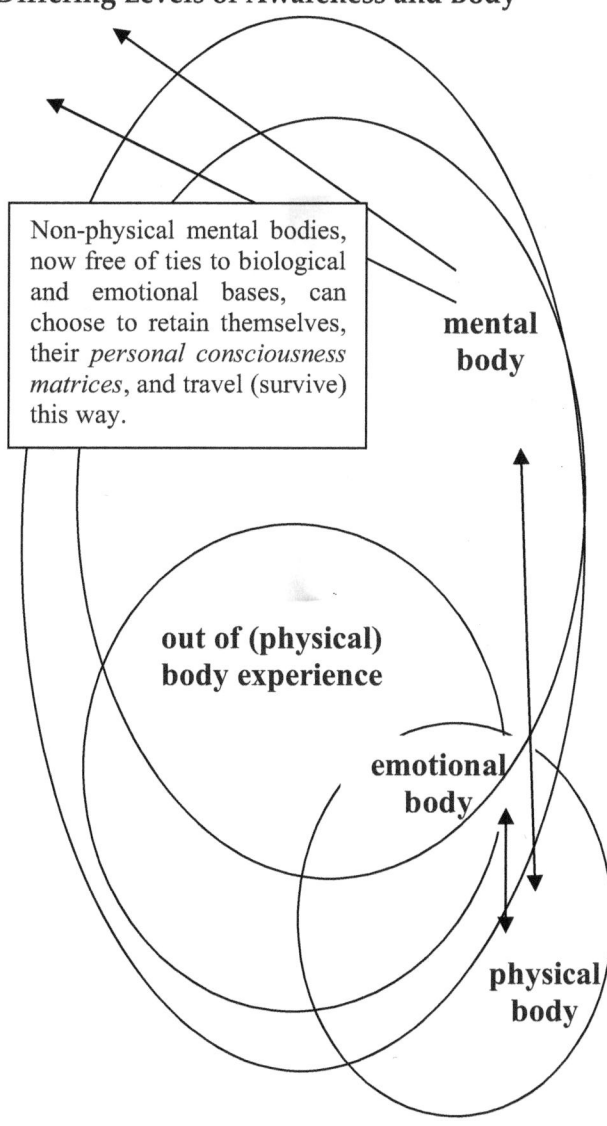

Physical, Emotional, and Mental Body Levels

BOOKLIST AND RECOMMENDED READING
Among the books in this
KEYS TO CONSCIOUSNESS AND SURVIVAL SERIES
by Dr. Angela Brownemiller:

Volume 9
Navigating Life's Stuff – Dynamics of Personal Change, Book <u>Two</u>
Keys to Consciously Moving Through Our Processes and Their Patterns
****

Volume 8
Navigating Life's Stuff – Dynamics of Personal Change, Book <u>One</u>
Sensitizing to and Navigating Our Patterns and Their Processes
****

Volume 7
The Go Conscious Process:
Steps and Practices for Heightening Conscious Awareness,
Shifts, Transmigrations of Focus,
LEAPS OF SELF
****

Volume 6
Overriding the Extinction Scenario, Part <u>Two</u>:
Raising the Bar on the Evolution of the Human Species
****

Volume 5
Overriding the Extinction Scenario, Part <u>One</u>:
Detecting the Bar on the Evolution of the Human Species
****

Volume 4
How to Die and Survive:
Interdimensional Psychology, Consciousness,
and Survival: Concepts for Living and Dying
****

Volume 3
Unveiling the Hidden Instinct:
Understanding Our
Interdimensional Survival Awareness
****

Volume 2
Keys to Self:
Your Next Steps to YOU
****

Volume 1
Keys to Personal Discovery:
Primer for Life's Minor and Major Challenges and Passages

BOOKLIST AND RECOMMENDED READING
Continued....

Ask Dr. Angela Series
Dr. Angela Brownemiller

The Politics of Perception
Dr. Angela Brownemiller

The Bloodwin Code
Dr. Angela Brownemiller

Earth Emergency
Dr. Angela Brownemiller

Transcending Addiction
Dr. Angela Brownemiller

Gestalting Addiction
Dr. Angela Brownemiller

Contact us for information on the special
Science Fiction Series
on these consciousness and survival topics.
Email:
DrAngela@DrAngela.com

Note:
These books should be listed on Amazon.com and numerous other book distributor websites. If not finding these books on these sites and or in book stores, request these bookstores order these books, and or contact Amazon.com or Metaterra® Publications at Metaterra.com and/or DrAngela@DrAngela.com or the author, Dr. Angela Brownemiller. Check also under last name, Browne-Miller. Thank you.

ABOUT THE AUTHOR
Dr. Angela Brownemiller
Dr. Angela®

Dr. Angela Brownemiller, also known as Dr. Angela®, is an author, journalist, social thinker, clinician, psychotherapist, trainer, speaker, and creator of the ASK DR. ANGELA Series of broadcasts, podcasts, books, audiobooks, Ebooks, and programs.. The views of Angela Brownemiller are centered on the great potential of the Human mind, heart, and soul, and on the rights of all of us, who and whatever we are (or think we are). Angela Brownemiller views the Human consciousness as a wealth of opportunity for exploration, insight, knowledge—and survival. For more information on her work, see DrAngela.com and AskDrAngela.Help

The works of Angela Brownemiller are brought to you by:
METATERRA® PUBLICATIONS
(and numerous other publishers, see Amazon.com).

For copies of this and other books by this author,
see Amazon.com
or contact us at
Info@Metaterra.com

To locate books listed on the previous pages,
see also Amazon.com or contact us at
Info@Metaterra.com

To take part in our events and workshops,
contact us at

DrAngela.com
DrAngela@DrAngela.com
For personal consultations
in person or by telephone,
contact us at
DrAngela@DrAngela.com

KEYS TO CONSCIOUSLY MOVING THROUGH OUR PROCESSES AND THEIR PATTERNS

GET THE TRUTH ABOUT ADDICTION

Life-changing insights into the reality of patterns, habits, addictions, and obsessions in our lives and minds.

Now in powerfully narrated AUDIOBOOK as well as PAPERBACK and EBOOK forms!

SEEING THE HIDDEN FACE OF ADDICTION
can be found on Amazon.com
and at http://www.DrAngela.com

Can we better understand the journeys we travel through in our lives? Can we detect and work with the patterns and processes we are forming, living within, and moving through? How much can we see about the patterns we form, and sometimes feel we cannot change, are caught in? How do we sensitize ourselves to the patterning processes we are engaged in? Find your way through the maze of life. See:

NAVIGATING LIFE'S STUFF:
DYNAMICS OF PERSONAL CHANGE, BOOK ONE
Seeing Our Processes and Their Patterns

NAVIGATING LIFE'S STUFF:
DYNAMICS OF PERSONAL CHANGE, BOOK TWO
Keys to Consciously Moving Through
Our Passages and Their Patterns

Now in Paperback, Audiobook, and Ebook forms.
Find these and other books by Dr. Angela Brownemiller
on Amazon.com and at DrAngela.com….

See the
ASK DR. ANGELA SERIES

A deep look at ourselves,
our minds, our brains, our lives.

See
AskDrAngela.help
And
DrAngela.com

For list of books
(Paperbacks, Audiobooks, Ebooks),
also workshops, and consult opportunities,
in this
ASK DR. ANGELA SERIES
By Angela Brownemiller.
DrAngela.com
Amazon.com

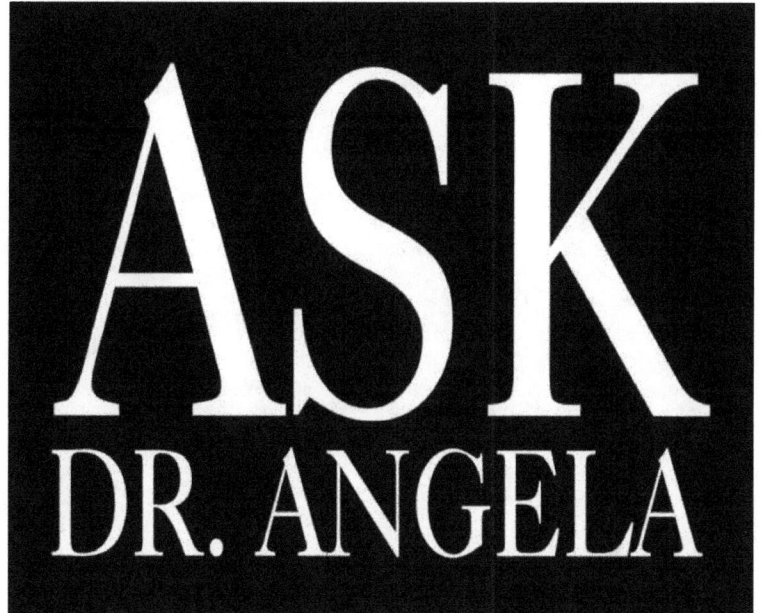

www.ingramcontent.com/pod-product-compliance
Lightning Source LLC
Chambersburg PA
CBHW062225080426
42734CB00010B/2034